THE
LOVING
TOUCH:

ENHANCING MALE
SEXUAL TECHNIQUE

THE LOVING TOUCH:

ENHANCING MALE SEXUAL TECHNIQUE

by James Wagenvoord
and Douglas Gasner

Ballantine Books • New York

Created and Produced by James Wagenvoord Studio, Inc.

Designed by David Larkin

Acknowledgments:

Special appreciation to Dr. Robert Bobrow
for his medical expertise in
reviewing the text, to Robert Nathan
for his generous assistance and timely support,
Ken Johnson for his insight, and to Toby Chiu,
Dr. Joseph Bohlen, Dr. Benjamin Graber, Dr. Julia R. Heiman,
Dr. Joseph LoPiccolo, Dr. John Money, Dr. William H. Masters,
Dr. James M. Murphy, Dr. Don Sloan

Library of Congress Catalog Card Number: 83-91163
ISBN 0-345-31464-6

Manufactured in the United States of America

First Ballantine Books Edition: August 1984

10   9   8   7   6   5   4   3   2   1

Contents

"When intercourse is good, even when it's just acceptable, I feel like I've had a really good talk with him. It's really a back-and-forth thing, where your feelings are communicated and so are his. It is called intercourse, after all."

Total
Involvement

Growing up we learn what it supposedly means to be a man. Men are strong. Men take charge. Men don't cry—or for that matter tremble, or show any of the so-called soft emotions. And above all, men dominate in bed, and women beg for more. Unfortunately, these simple axioms don't always seem to work.

Most men, after all, don't always feel strong. And who doesn't occasionally, if not often, wish someone else would take charge?

You have undoubtedly run up against some of the contradictions between the conventional idea of manhood and your own sense of yourself. This book takes off from the assumption that you're ready to go on doing so, in the interest of turning lovemaking into as complete and fulfilling an experience as it can possibly be. By coming to terms with the softer emotions, especially in bed, you'll experience some of the most important aspects of intimacy. And by sharing the insights of men and women who were interviewed during the writing of this book, you'll find out firsthand what's actually going on during intercourse and what it takes to be a better lover.

Along the way some of your illusions about sex will be shattered, because if you're like most of us, you have rarely if ever had frankly candid conversations with anyone, men or women, about the actual experience of sex, particularly the act of intercourse. The synonyms and acronyms are used, the buzzwords repeated, but insights about techniques and attitudes are not shared. There may be no taboo, but the fact is we simply don't discuss it. And most of us continue to go with our instincts.

These days the instincts simply aren't enough to allow a man and his partner the intimate sharing that the moment has to offer. The trial and error of all those who have preceded us haven't added one iota of sexual experience to our genes. We have no more of a head start as good lovers than our Victorian ancestors had. The social climate may be more or less permissive, but each of us has to take the first step.

This book will give you authoritative answers to the intimate questions about sex—especially about intercourse. It focuses on intercourse for three reasons:

★ In intercourse the greatest pleasures are available to you and your partner;

★ The magical bond that sexuality creates between two people is most heightened in intercourse;

★ New discoveries in sex research can be applied to enhancing your technique.

No book, of course, can turn you into a great lover

overnight. Great lovers bring more than technique into bed. Nor can a book change you into a better husband or a more sensitive human being. This is not an attempt to solve all the problems in your life or a manual of complicated sexual exercises requiring months of practice. But learning about the latest discoveries in sex research can change the quality of your lovemaking.

Because this book is not designed to totally reform anyone's life, a few assumptions are made about you. It is assumed that you are not troubled by exaggerated sexual guilt and are open to new sexual experiences. It is assumed that you are willing to learn about your body and how it works; that you enjoy relatively good health and consume a varied and reasonably balanced diet; and that you do not use drugs or alcohol to excess. And it is assumed that you'll try to break through whatever personal barriers you might have built against your own ability to experience pleasure.

As authors, we don't have any values to sell. We don't advocate any rules or endorse a particular lifestyle. If there is any bias at all, it's in favor of exploring the potential of our sexuality.

If a woman walked up to you on a street corner and asked where to find the nearest grocery store, you would tell her. "Down the block, take a left past the post office." But if she asked you in French, you might shake your head and try to explain you only spoke English.

Why? Isn't language natural?

Language is natural only to the extent that you can learn it. The same is true for sexual behavior. It's mostly learned.

We do have an instinct to reproduce, and we have a natural desire for pleasure—what Freud called the pleasure principle, our tendency to repeat gratifying experiences. Anthropologists tell us that certain sexual habits, like flirting, and our responses to certain stimuli, like women's breasts, have been bred into us by evolution. Even the relative hairlessness of our bodies—compared, for instance, to those of apes—may have been nature's way of making us more attractive to one another. How we make love, however, varies from culture to culture. The Eskimos, for example, choose their sexual partners in a game called "douse the lights." In one Tanzanian tribe the idea of romantic love in marriage is scoffed at; marriage is accepted as a business deal and everyone has secret lovers on the side. In France, according to one well-publicized poll, the first thing a man does after sex is call home. Whatever the passage of time may have done for us, the way we seek our pleasure—choose our partners, express ourselves in bed—is to a large extent learned.

We've told ourselves, too, that men and women are irrevocably different, and as a consequence we harbor odd notions about sex, many of which we'd deny if anybody asked us. We know they're foolish, but they've been in our heads so long, become so entrenched in our view of the world, that we can't exorcise them. They take many forms. Women hunger for sex and men don't, or men hunger for it and women shouldn't. If she does, then she's somebody to be used. If we do, we're real men. If we don't, we're not. Some men are prey to what's called the whore-madonna complex, in which it's all right to lust after some women and love others, but never to feel both lust and love for the same person.

What we know about sex depends on where we learned about it and who taught us. Our parents, television, popular fiction, movies, the streetcorner—we get bits of information, much of it inaccurate, from each of these sources. If we all lived in the world of television, for instance, most of the women we met would be voluptuous, sex-starved heiresses, kindly mothers and grandmothers, or the girl next door. And as lovers we would be nothing more than what one woman calls wrigglers-and-pokers: "They climb on, wriggle around, poke a few times, and climb off."

Finally, we take our economic role into the bedroom. We think it's our responsibility to provide the proverbial groceries.

In this scenario, her needs outweigh ours. A voice from within keeps repeating, "Make sure she gets off." If a woman doesn't, most men are left with a sense of inadequacy, if not failure. Whether we "get off," and *how* we get off, become irrelevant.

Our sense of failure develops from all the definitions of manhood we've received, not to mention the messages our society gives women. Women, too, have been inhibited by our provider role and get caught in false assumptions about what is right and wrong. A woman can feel constrained if she, too, believes that a good lover is solely responsible for her orgasms. It's little wonder we sometimes feel trapped. But who put us in this trap in the first place? We did, along with a lot of help from the society we grew up in, and only we can get ourselves out.

A good lover is not solely a provider of orgasms.

Yes, women want orgasms, but they don't necessarily consider sex a washout without one. In the past

13

twenty years, women have become far more sophisticated about sex than men—partly because of open communication fostered by the women's movement, and partly because from childhood on women are encouraged to experience their own sensuality, behavior our culture doesn't generally consider masculine. Women in general today address issues of sexuality with far more candor than men do. As a consequence many men have some catching up to do. From the opposite sex's point of view, being a good lover these days clearly entails a lot more than merely having a penis. Here's what some of the women interviewed during the writing of this book had to say about intercourse:

On Penetration

Janet K., age 29
> At the very beginning, when he's first inside, there's a moment of extreme pleasure for me. Sometimes, not often, he lets me guide his penis in, sometimes he just seems to know when. Sometimes it seems magical, it just goes in by itself, it's more intimate and makes the penetration part of the lovemaking instead of something that's done to me. The quality of the sensation, other than the purely physical feeling of pressure and wanting to have something inside, filling me up—the quality is incredibly restful and still, this sense of completion in the first few seconds after he enters me. It's very calm and enormously fulfilling, just feeling him

fill that space. It feels like I've always wanted somebody to be doing that, and now for a few short moments I'm getting exactly what I want —with him doing nothing other than entering me.

Ann B., age 30
When a man enters, it's like everything has been building to this. It's like getting the candy. It's like you're a pulled rubber band, in anticipation, and then you relax. Your body takes over. It's like the twenty-mile limit, when you're running, and you break through. Your body begins to move and your emotions and your body are all working together.

On Arousal

Sally L., age 26
When I'm having sex with someone I love, there's a time when I'm here, meaning on the bed, and then there's a time when it builds up and I go off into never-never land.

Rita M., age 38
There is a certain mechanism to building toward orgasm, a certain rhythm. If a man's focusing, if he's involved, if he understands that and is willing to take the time and read you, he can do that, build a rhythm. One of things I don't like is men who are so concentrated on

giving me pleasure that they stop and start, stop and start, just because they think delaying will make me happy. It would, but not done like that. I'd rather have it short and right. If they're just delaying for the sake of delay, they're not reading my needs. But if they're delaying and can keep up the rhythm, it can be terrific. You have to read each other, you have to be in touch. If the man is somewhere else, I can tell. I hate that more than anything else. If he comes, okay, we'll do it again later, but this start-stop stuff is awful.

Toward Orgasm

Odette G., age 19

It isn't just one person there, it's him and me in that particular act, and so what makes a good lover is someone who's *there*. If we move together, if he's there with me, it doesn't matter specifically how he moves. Sometimes I want him to move really fast and hard, sometimes I don't. Sometimes it's fabulous, I want him to go up the whole way to my throat. But not if that's *all* he does. I slept with a man once, more than once, who was a pounder. That was all he knew how to do. And I didn't enjoy it. That was his bit, that was his standard move. And if he's not with me, then he's not making love. He's masturbating inside of me.

Connie S., age 29

I get tense if I think he's bored waiting for me to come. If a man could sometimes make it clear —somehow let me know—"hey don't rush, we've got plenty of time, we've got all day," then I think I'd feel better. Not every time, but once in a while. Sometimes if he'd wait just a little while longer, just another minute or two, I'd get there. I can't ask him afterward to help me get an orgasm, even though I'd like to.

On Clitoral Stimulation

Beth F., age 34

Most men I've slept with don't really know where the clitoris is. They're too far down or too far up. And they don't know how to rub, they rub too hard. I don't tell them, because it's embarrassing. It's probably embarrassing for them to ask, but if they did, I'd tell them. It'd be nice if they'd ask. Of course the question is how to do it nicely—with your hand. Without saying anything it's very hard for all of us, I think.

Lori O., age 31

What I like is when my lover goes in and out —not really thrusting—and each time he goes in he moves up, in and up, then out, in and up, then out, because that way I get clitoral stimulation, too. It's an incredibly small difference, but it's amazing what a big difference it makes. His technique makes me more responsive during intercourse because it changes my temperature, muscle tone, everything.

Joanne A., Age 30

They keep saying there's no difference between a vaginal orgasm and a clitoral orgasm, and in my experience that just isn't true. A vaginal orgasm is a very special thing. If you're in the right frame of mind, the right "head" to have it, then no matter what's going on physically, you can have a different experience that you feel vaginally and not clitorally. It's a deeper, more satisfying orgasm and has nothing to do with orgasms you get through other kinds of activities that don't include intercourse. I'm not talking about a different quality of orgasm, it's a totally different experience. It is nothing like the orgasm I get by masturbating. It's much, much more intense, with feelings of tenderness and closeness afterwards.

Candy B., age 21

I don't have any idea what they're talking about, these women who talk about vaginal orgasm. But I do find vaginal stimulation pleasant. The real overall pleasure, though, comes from clitoral stimulation for me. If there's anything I'd confuse with a vaginal orgasm, it's the rush I get when a man comes.

Donna P., age 32

I think I believe in vaginal orgasm. Once I got it from the outside—my lover was pressing on my pelvis—and it did feel different. In general, though, ninety-nine percent of my orgasms are clitoral. And I need clitoral stimulation. It's hard to get, and the only position I get it in is on top.

Liza L., age 34

When I do have an orgasm during intercourse, bells go off, it's fabulous.

Barbara T., age 36

In my experience, unless I get some kind of manual clitoral stimulation during inter-course, it's very difficult to come. His timing and activity usually have more to do with the outcome. For me, anyway.

On Orgasm

Suzanne L., age 33

It doesn't matter so much. I mean, I like to come, but it's satisfying even if I don't. You know, it's arousing to give somebody else pleasure.

Karen R., age 28

There are definitely some men who go deeper and deeper during their partner's orgasm because some woman told them to do it once, and they've been doing it ever since. When it works for me, it's because my lover seems to be able to move to the same rhythm as my vaginal contractions, and he stays inside until my contractions have stopped because he knows it feels better for me when my vagina is contracting around his penis.

Janis J., age 29

If I felt that having orgasms was the only reason to have intercourse, then I'd never have sex. And I like sex. To get greedy about it, of course I want orgasms every time. But I don't count on it. I feel an enormous release from intercourse anyway. If I'm really tense when I start, I'm really relaxed when I'm done.

Knowing how a woman responds during intercourse, and what her needs are, is only half the equation. Women think differently from men, more "globally," as the educational psychologist Eleanor Maccoby puts it—the big picture before the details. They want sensitivity to their needs, and they want to be sensitive to yours.

While you might at first be turned on more quickly by visual stimuli, she favors tactile sensations more. While you might derive sensual pleasure from thrusting, she gets turned on more by the rhythm. While you might not think of slowing down, she likes to savor all the delights. She likes to feel the penis almost come out and then go back in, sometimes slowly, sometimes quickly.

You can feel her respond, the caress of her labia, the ridges and valleys along her vaginal walls, the tensing of her muscles as your penis is held, then released —all the sounds, sights, and smells that makes sex a feast, not fast food.

We are living in an age of instant gratification, and unfortunately sex gets shortchanged along with other pleasurable activities that ordinarily take time to learn to enjoy. The rise in the consumption of vodka is a case in point. This distillate takes on the taste of anything you mix it with—so one never has to acquire a taste for the flavored alcohols to get the effects. Instant gratification. Somehow lost in the mix are the subtleties—the bouquet, the aroma, the aftertaste— that can make imbibing more than a way to get drunk or diminish inhibitions. Similarly, instant gratification sex leaves a lot to be desired.

It also leaves a good many men and women under the blankets but out in the cold.

The New Physiology

Anatomy, Freud told us, is destiny. In the half century since the great Viennese psychiatrist uttered this judgment, it has taken on all sorts of meanings he never intended.

Not the least substantive of these is that in some sense an unbridgeable chasm separates the sexes because our genitals are so different. Women have their needs—stemming from their anatomy—needs totally separate from and unrelated to men's.

Medical research has given the lie to this misconception. Male and female anatomical parts, it turns out, are more similar than they look; the chasm between the sexes would more accurately be described as a small gulf.

What Freud meant, by the way, is that anatomy, both men's and women's, is one of the causes of shame

HOMOLOGY

From left to right, the development of the male and female external genitals, enlarged in the drawings for detail, from one-and-a-half months to birth: the stages show how similar tissue develops differently in the sexes due to the influence of the Y chromosome.

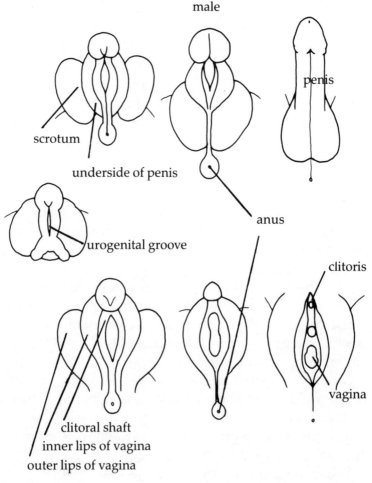

male

penis

scrotum

underside of penis

anus

urogenital groove

clitoris

clitoral shaft
inner lips of vagina
outer lips of vagina

vagina

female

about sex. The organs of sexual pleasure, by natural design, either function with or lie close to the organs for excretion. As William Butler Yeats put it, "Love has pitched his mansion in the place of excrement."

Not understanding more about our anatomy may be only one thread in the general fabric of our misplaced sexual bravado—"I don't care how it works as long as I get it up"—but here is one area where ignorance most assuredly isn't bliss. And in this case ignorance can actually deny you the bliss you're searching for.

You'll begin to see how small the anatomical difference is when you realize that what you have on the outside, she has on the inside. (This is not quite literally the case, but it's closer to the truth than you probably think.) In a very special sense, your sexual equipment and hers have exactly the same embryonic origin.

During the first six to seven weeks of life, a human embryo shows no observable gender. It has the potential to become male or female. The determination, of course, was made when the egg was fertilized by a sperm bearing either an X chromosome for a girl or a Y chromosome for a boy.

At the bidding of specific genes carried on the X or the Y chromosome, the sexual organs take shape; a particular group of cells grows into either male or female genitals. The penis, for example, develops from the same tissue that would become the clitoris. What becomes the scrotum would turn into the outer lips of the vagina, the labia majora, in a woman. The tissue that forms the underside of the penis and extends rearward to encircle the anus has as its counterpart the inner lips of the vagina. The testicles, which develop internally and descend into the scrotum several months before birth, share the same origin as the ovaries. Because male and female external sex organs are homologous (the scientific term for structures derived from the same material in the development of the embryo), virtually every area of a man's genitals has a corresponding structure in a woman.

MALE SEXUAL ANATOMY

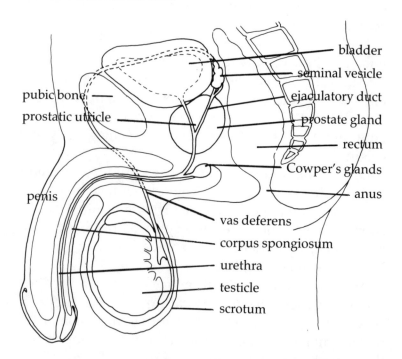

Some of the similarities are easy to recognize, those between the clitoris and the penis being the most obvious. Both are extraordinarily sensitive to the touch.

Both grow erect during sexual arousal. And both are central to the experience of orgasm. You might presume, on the assumption that bigger is better, that the penis is more sensitive than the clitoris. This is not the case, for the number of nerve endings—which transmit physical sensations—is equally large in both. The nerve endings in the clitoris are simply clustered in a smaller area, which is why the clitoris responds to touch as powerfully as the penis, if not more so.

What may not be so apparent is the similarity between the vagina and a tiny mound of tissue in the male called the prostatic utricle. They don't look alike, but both are derived from an embryonic structure called the urogenital sinus. The prostatic utricle is a small pouch beside the prostate gland, which is below the bladder and near the rectum. Two ducts, one from each testicle, merge with the ducts from the seminal vesicles (two small sacs behind the bladder, which eject fluid that in turn activates the sperm's swimming mechanism) as they enter the prostate to form the paired inch-long ejaculatory ducts within the body of the gland itself. Secretions from the prostate gland are discharged during ejaculation into the urethra, the final conduit of semen on its way to being ejected through the penis. As for the small pouchlike utricle, it has what physicians call no clinical significance—no known purpose.

The existence of the prostatic utricle, however, and its derivation from the same tissue as the vagina, do have significance for male sexual response, identifying what may well be the master erogenous zone in men.

In 1950 a German gynecologist named Ernst Grafenberg described an erotic area in the vagina that had never before been mentioned in the annals of sexual literature. Grafenberg also asserted that during orgasm women experience ejaculation, somewhat similar to men's. At the time psychiatrists and medical researchers had little factual information on female orgasm and gave virtually no credence to Grafenberg's claims.

For reasons that probably have more to do with cultural attitudes than with scientific veracity, sex research has always been an uphill battle. Any gains are met with resistance; once accepted, however, theories are held to be inviolable dogma. Thus the battle must be joined again and again.

The recent popularization of Grafenberg's research, with the area he identified now named the G-spot, has brought forth a host of supporters and nay-sayers. Although women, doctors, and sex researchers are still debating Grafenberg's work, current research seems to verify both the existence of both the G-spot and female ejaculation.

The G-spot, located in the upper anterior (front) wall of the vagina, appears to be sensitive only because of a structure lying behind it, a hummock of tissue that has the capacity to enlarge during arousal. Exactly what this tissue is and what purpose it serves are open to speculation, but it is believed to develop from the same embryonic tissue that becomes the prostate in the male. Many women report that stimulating this area sometimes produces "deeper" and more powerful orgasms than they experience from only clitoral stimulation.

Until recently sex research focused mainly on women. One reason was the long-held assumption,

FEMALE SEXUAL ANATOMY

G-SPOT

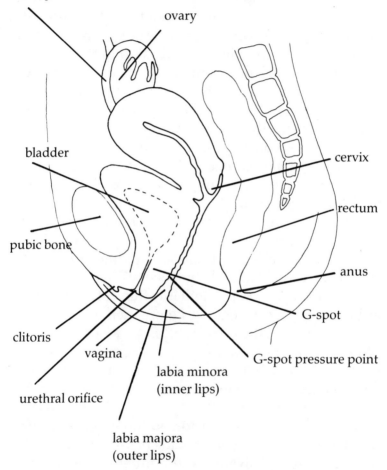

The G-spot, a mass of variable density tissue around the upper urethra, where it merges with the neck of the bladder, can be felt manually from the inside of the vagina during arousal when it tends to increase in size and hardness.

even among medical researchers, that women's sexuality is more complicated than men's. In one sense this assumption is correct. There is no obvious biological reason for women to experience orgasm, which is only to say that a woman doesn't need to have an orgasm to get pregnant. The female orgasm is a learned response. If it had a direct connection to the survival of the species, sex researchers say, it would be apparent earlier in women, when in fact it increases with practice and age. Men, on the other hand, must ejaculate in order for the species to reproduce itself.

Another reason for the focus of sex research on women is that the researchers have generally been men. However objective men might be, their personalities, including both curiosity about women and anxiety about their own sexual roles, may have steered them toward studying women.

The greatest obstacle to understanding either male or female sexuality has been society's taboos against sexual knowledge. We customarily think of sex research as beginning in this century. Before then, we suppose, everyone lived in the Dark Ages. Sex was a dirty secret. No one understood the physiology of arousal or orgasm. And the idea of sex as a form of mutual pleasure between two people we consider an invention of our enlightened times.

As it happens, some doctors in the nineteenth century tried to break through the fog of Victorian morality. In 1899 a paper delivered to the fiftieth annual meeting of the American Medical Association described the physiology of sex and the pleasure available to both men and women. Dr. Denslow Lewis, author of the paper, noted the erection of the clitoris and the "pleasurable sensation" when the penis entered the vagina. He asked doctors to explain that a man is "not the master but the companion of his wife. . . . There should be no tyranny or assumption of superiority in a matter like the sexual act, which is vital to the happiness of each partner." But when Lewis submitted his work for publication in the *Journal of the American Medical Association*, he was turned down. In rejecting the article, George H. Simmons, the *Journal* editor, said that any discussion of sex "is attended with more or less filth and we besmirch ourselves by discussing it in public." Even as recently as twenty-five years ago, according to a recent report in a sex journal, half of the students graduating from Philadelphia's medical schools believed masturbation caused mental illness; 20 percent of their professors did, too.

But all that is changing, and men, too, can benefit from the increasing attention being given to unraveling the mysteries of their sexual experience. The benefits can translate into substantial improvements in performance and pleasure. Men often joke that one orgasm is like another. "Bad sex? What could be bad about it?" Admittedly, describing sexual experiences presents us with the same problem the poet Paul Valery perceived in his craft: "Everything which must be said is almost impossible to say well." But we have all experienced sex that is, if not bad, just mediocre. If you're not in the mood, if you're busy performing instead of enjoying, if you're partner is unresponsive—well, you may ejaculate, but you may feel afterward that the episode hardly justified the effort. Indeed, some men who find sex invariably unexciting or unsatisfying get so bored they swear off regular sex altogether. But one orgasm need not necessarily be like another, and there's no reason for sex to become boring.

Among the ways to keep sex from becoming boring is to explore your own body's responses—to discover how you are aroused, to involve your partner, and to become more comfortable experiencing sexual pleasure beyond sensations in the penis.

Beth F., age 34:
> Men close down a part of their body as not sexual. If they'll take the time, they'll find that I can touch them in places that are wonderfully sensitive. But in order for that to be arousing, a man has to go with it. And some men are taken aback, they'll stop and turn off.

The latest medical discoveries show that men, too, have what can be considered an equivalent to the G-spot. It is located in a key erogenous zone called the Y-zone.

Picture the area below your penis as a Y. The two sides of the scrotum form the arms of the Y, meeting in a single line that extends back toward the anus. The rear of the scrotum attaches to the perineum, an area of flesh marking the lowest boundary of the pelvis. Here, where the three arms of the Y intersect, is a man's equivalent to the G-spot, which we will call the PG-point. The letters stand for "prostate gland." Since the prostatic utricle, as mentioned earlier, is analogous to the vagina in its development, the sexual importance of the prostate area shouldn't come as a complete surprise.

The prostate gland manufactures part of the fluid that carries sperm. The gland itself, normally no larger

than a walnut but considerably softer, is passively contracted by surrounding muscles to help expel semen
just prior to ejaculation. Some researchers believe that
the G-spot is homologous to the prostate gland; this
would account for female ejaculation.

Y-ZONE

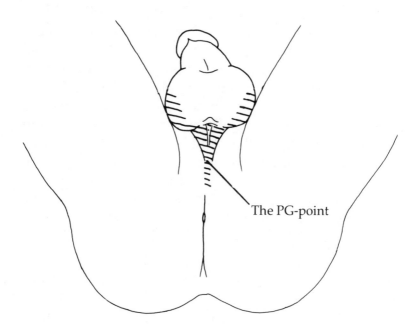

The PG-point

A man's most intimate experience with the prostate
usually comes at his annual physical checkup, when
the doctor inserts a plastic-gloved finger into the anus
and pushes up quite firmly to check the prostate's
condition. Enlargement or hardening of the prostate
can indicate an infection or a malignancy. And because

33

the urethra, the tube that carries urine from the kidneys, passes through the prostate, any abnormal changes in the prostate's structure can impede the flow of urine.

Medical examination of the prostate is invasive, not to mention downright uncomfortable. How, then, can stimulation of this gland be sexually arousing? That's not only a fair question, it's an important one. Bear in mind that the subject is stimulation, and indirect stimulation at that—not examination. There is a direct connection between the prostate gland and male sexual function. Direct massage of the prostate gland can cause sperm to be expressed spontaneously; that is, without ejaculation. In animal breeding programs, the prostates of bulls and stallions are stimulated electronically with special probes, and the semen is collected for later use in artificial insemination. The prostate is intimately involved in men's sexual experience as well. But traditionally the gland itself has been thought to have no sexual sensitivity, and since it lies deep inside the body, it is relatively inaccessible to direct stimulation.

Recent research has expanded the understanding of the prostate's role, particularly in showing that branches of the pelvic nerve, which serve the prostate, can participate in arousal, along with sensory fibers of the pudendal nerve that lie close to the surface of the Y-zone. The mechanism is twofold: the sensory nerve endings are responsive to tactile stimulation, and in a chain of related nervous-system events the progression of nerve excitement that transmits the arousal message to the brain also prepares the prostate for its involvement in the sexual scenario. Many men responding to questionnaires for *The Hite Report On Male Sexuality* described stimulation of the prostate as increasing the intensity of orgasm.

To understand why the PG-point, which lies along the two-to-three-inch span of the Y-zone, is sensitive, we have to refer once again to embryonic development. The Y-zone is known in the parlance of anatomical description as a raphe, a place where two sides of the body, roughly symmetrical, are welded together. (Other raphes, for example, are at the center of the tongue, down the middle of the back, and of course on the penis and scrotum.) Along every such seam on the body lie clusters of nerve receptors, making the seams quite sensitive to touch.

PROSTATIC UTRICLE

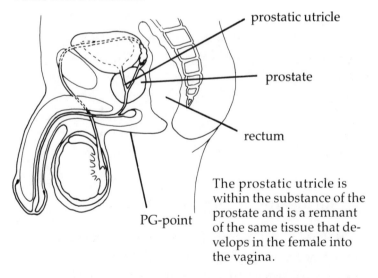

prostatic utricle

prostate

rectum

PG-point

The prostatic utricle is within the substance of the prostate and is a remnant of the same tissue that develops in the female into the vagina.

The critical importance of the nerve endings around the PG-point was recently discovered by two doctors investigating the aftermath of prostate surgery. A vast array of events must take place for a man to have an erection and orgasm. One of these is the trapping of blood in the erectile tissues of the penis, a collection of three separate cylindrical bodies. Dr. Patrick Walsh of the Johns Hopkins Hospital and Dr. Pieter Donker of the University of Leiden in the Netherlands reported that the nerves that control the blood flow by contracting or dilating the muscles in the walls of the arteries in two of these cylinders—the *corpora cavernosa*—lie near the PG-point. The importance of these nerves was demonstrated when they were severed during surgery and, in most cases, the patient became impotent. It's clear, then, that the PG-point has a very direct connection to the physical sensations of sex.

Using the PG-point to Increase Your Pleasure

We suggest here two exercises using the PG-point to enhance your lovemaking. The exercises are for you. If you're not accustomed to concentrating completely on your own pleasure, ask your partner to help you; remember that women get pleasure from your pleasure.

1. Exploring the PG-point Alone

Set aside some time for yourself, preferably in a place where you won't be disturbed. If necessary, ask your partner to leave you alone for a while—no calls, no questions about supper. Masturbate until you feel close to ejaculating, but not so close that you can't stop. Pause for a moment, then stroke along the Y-zone between the rear of your scrotum and your anus, concentrating on trying to find your most sensitive area, which will be your personal PG-point. For most men, it's not far along the bottom of the Y.

Now try a harder pressure in the same area for a moment and start masturbating again. Continue masturbating until you come, trying different amounts of pressure on your PG-point.

At different stages—when you're flaccid, when you're erect but not near ejaculation, and when you can feel the urge to come —you'll find that stroking and putting pressure on the PG-point cause different sensations. Many men find that light long strokes just before coming enhance the physiological state of arousal, while strong pressure just at the moment of orgasm intensifies the sensation throughout the pelvis.

2. The PG-point During Intercourse

Before intercourse, ask your partner to stroke the PG-point without ever touching your penis. If she starts with a firm stroke from the back of the scrotum along the bottom of the Y, you can tell her when she's reached the most sensitive spot.

Continue with your usual foreplay when *you* feel ready. Let your partner know in advance that you'll signal her. Using what you found in the first exercise, ask her to exert the kind of pressure you like on the PG-point as you begin intercourse, as you reach what feels like your height of excitement before orgasm, and as you come. You may not be able to make yourself clear the first time, but eventually your partner will understand what kind of stroking at the PG-point gives you the most pleasure.

If you find that talking during intercourse interrupts your pleasure—if you can't say, for example, "Harder now," or "A little farther back"—you can send messages by letting your excitement show in other ways. We tend to joke about moaning and sighing during sex; we think it's all right for women, but not for us. This is another one of those blocks we have against letting go. If you were playing a strenuous game of basketball or tennis, you'd think nothing of grunting. It's part of the rhythm of the game. And you might sigh to express satisfaction when you finish a difficult piece of work or, say, when you are having your back rubbed. There's nothing wrong with making noise when you're excited, and a moan comes quite naturally if you're in ecstasy. Let yourself express the pleasure.

Starting on page 120 you will find three suggestions for using the PG-point specifically to help control the timing of your orgasm.

The Mechanics of Arousal

Sexual arousal is the result of a combination of chemistry and psychology. The chemistry of sex is far from completely understood. It is clear that hormones called androgens, the most powerful among them being testosterone, are responsible for our sex drive. Testosterone affects not only our ability to ejaculate but our capacity for arousal as well. When cells deep in a region of the brain called the hypothalamus, which is associated with the libido, are artificially inhibited by certain drugs, the conscious imagery of sexual arousal fades. Men participating in sex research of this kind, who had previously been turned on by sexual fantasy or by one sexual image or another, find they are no longer aroused by the same stimulus. Sex researchers also have discovered both daily and weekly testosterone cycles in men, which may affect when we're interested in sex and when we're not. In women the evidence is more definitive; during a woman's monthly menstrual cycle, her body responds to the ebb and flow of the hormones estrogen and progesterone with sometimes profound emotional and physical changes, which may explain why she feels sexually responsive on some days and totally uninterested in sex on others.

Beth F., age 34:
There's nothing worse than having sex when you don't want to have it. There's no bigger

turnoff than when I allow myself to have sex when I'm not in the mood. I do it just to please him, not to have to fight, it's easier. But then it really repulses me. I guess I should be able to say no. I wish I could. I wish I could feel the freedom to say no, but I'm not there yet. I wonder if it's the same for men.

Ann B., age 30:
Intercourse can be disappointing, but I don't expect it to be perfect every time. If he's in a bad mood and isn't being considerate, I just want to quit. I'm even capable of generalizing from a bad night or a good night and saying that if the sex is good then the relationship is good. Sometimes it's true and sometimes it isn't. It's hard to know whether it's a self-fulfilling prophecy.

When you're in the mood and she isn't, or the other way around, accept that it takes two to enjoy making love; both her mood and yours may depend on physiological as well as emotional cues. If you're in an ongoing relationship, take heart from the belief of some researchers that partners who stay together for a long time may affect each other's hormonal cycles, though how this happens is still unexplained.

The mystery of hormones and sex is revealed in one astonishing recent discovery that explains why intercourse affects us as no other sexual experience can. Researchers have found that men who reached orgasm through masturbation had little increase in the levels of testosterone in their bloodstream, while men reaching orgasm through intercourse had a considerable increase in their hormonal levels. This increase correlates with a heightened sense of ecstasy and shows that men are capable of having more than one type of orgasm. An orgasm reached by masturbation may not be as powerful as an orgasm reached through intercourse. This research also calls into question the traditional idea that women's orgasms are always more overwhelming than men's.

As men get older, testosterone production begins a gradual but modest decline. When boys are in their late teens, their daily secretion of testosterone reaches its peak. A teenager's libido seems to be primed all the time, and he gets erections that seem never to go away. But when our days as priapic adolescents are over, we discover that we don't get emotionally aroused as quickly. Our erections may lag behind a bit, taking longer to grow completely hard. If once there was a time when we could perform on demand, without much stimulation, now it's not so easy.

A man recently confided a not uncommon sexual problem:"My wife is more in the mood than ever, but I don't get it up as fast or as often as I used to. It's scaring me so much I sometimes don't get it up at all." Both he and his wife are in their late thirties, and together they're discovering what at first seems to be an unfortunate accident of nature. It could be called the Inverted Triangles—a diagram of human sexual development.

At the very same time when men are on the downward slope of their triangle, women are at the top of theirs. Adolescent girls have barely begun to know the pleasures of orgasm, even though their hormones make them just as interested in sex as men are. But for women, having orgasms takes more than the right hormonal mixture and being interested; it takes practice. This is why many women don't begin to experience their full range of sexual sensations until their late twenties. Nature gives an extra advantage to women who have had children; their genitals reach higher levels of vasocongestion—more blood in the pelvic area—and thus higher levels of physical tension during intercourse, making their orgasms more intensely satisfying. The late twenties and early thirties also mark a psychological change in many women. They've begun to demolish many of their inhibitions against sexual pleasure. Told for many years that "nice girls don't," they decide that nice women most definitely do.

If you're inclined to consider the Inverted Triangles a disaster, they will be. You'll worry about getting erections, question your manhood when you don't, and undercut your own pleasure.

But the differing sexual cycles of men and women turn out to be a blessing. Young men can ejaculate quickly, but too often that's all sex is. What do they know of tenderness, of prolonged physical intimacy, of the rewards of languorous lovemaking? As you grow older, you can sustain your erections longer with greater ease. You can enjoy the sensual pleasures of intercourse, allow your arousal to build with heightened sexual tension, and often find orgasm an even more fulfilling release. Best of all, you can make love better because we can relax and take your time.

Mind Over Matter

No matter how fully primed the libido or how experienced you or your lover may be, you can still stop yourself from becoming aroused. If you're angry, or feeling pressured to have sex when you don't want to, or simply exhausted from stress, you'll turn off. This is why it's often said that the most important organ in sex isn't your penis, it's your brain; as John Lennon put it, "It's all in your head." We tend to think it's outside influences that turn us on, and while this is partly true, we have more control over the process than we think. Desire may manifest itself in an erection, but it starts a few inches under the skull.

If the brain is the most important organ in sex, what's the second? You might assume it's the penis, but you'd be wrong. According to recent research, it's your skin, and not only the skin on your genitals. If you were in a state of extreme arousal with a receptive partner, the touch of her fingers anywhere on your body would be sufficient to bring you to the edge of ejaculation. Because men traditionally have not been able to simply relax and luxuriate in sensuous skin caresses, they are generally unaware of how sensitive the skin is all over the body. Women understand how critical touch is to arousal:

Rita M., age 38:
I think there's something people overlook, and in fact it's just a straightforward biological phenomenon. It's why the "zipless fuck," the

43

fast sex with someone you don't know, has always played this fantasy role in the back of our sexual consciousness. It's a matter of arousal. I don't care who you're with, but if you're worked to a lather, then all systems are go, then all kinds of tactile stimulation make a difference. The problem with being with someone you're used to is that you can't reach a fever pitch unless you're trying something new. And when it's good, it's like exploding walls, just incredible.

The Path
to Orgasm

The specific feelings that accompany arousal and orgasm are different for every man. But the physical aspects of sex—how a man's body actually reaches orgasm—are the same for all. Various kinds of stimulation can cause an erection: thoughts, fantasies, a kiss, a quick stroke of the thigh. Whatever the trigger, a message is sent to the brain through the autonomic, or involuntary, nervous system. The message returns to the lower sections of the spine, where the *nervi erigentes*, nerves of erection (better known as the pelvic nerves), receive it. This in turn sets off the process of erection, a grand feat of hydraulic engineering. Blood flows into soft cylinders of spongy tissue in the penis.

As the penis engorges, blood vessels with valves regulate the pressure until there is sufficient blood to maintain erection—eight times the amount of blood found in a flaccid penis. If everything is working, the penis stays erect. Recent research, revealing previously undescribed shunt vessels that hold the blood in the penis, shows just how delicate this process is. In fact, when you consider how many precisely timed changes have to occur, it's one of nature's little miracles that we get erections at all.

The length of time you can stay aroused depends on the kind of stimulation you get, both physical and emotional. But during that time, your body passes through several distinct, recognizable levels of arousal. The first is excitement. In the second level, called the plateau phase, the head of your penis, called the corona, may darken in color to a light purple as a result of the blood held under pressure in the veins. The skin on your scrotum may tighten. Your testicles will grow roughly 50 percent larger as the vessels engorge with blood, and eventually they'll start rising toward your body as involuntary muscles in the spermatic cords tighten; both you and your partner can read these signals to control your pace toward orgasm.

You might notice other changes. Your entire body may display evidence of increasing sexual arousal—a pink flush coloring your chest, faster heartbeat and more rapid breathing. And a small amount of pre-ejaculatory fluid, secreted by the Cowper's glands (two pea-sized structures at the base of the penis), appears at the end of the penis; although it's not semen, it may contain sperm. Its function is to neutralize the acidity of any residual urine and to lubricate the urethra in preparation for ejaculation.

No one has yet discovered the exact physiological trigger for ejaculation—precisely what takes a man from being on the edge to the event itself. Any man, of course, knows when it's been set off, and eventually can control the timing of his orgasm to some extent by recognizing the moment just before the trigger is pulled. The ability to perceive sensations in the genitals is one of the reasons we can control, to one degree or another, when we ejaculate. Once you become more familiar with these sensations, consciously manipulating the PG-point and the side arms of the Y-zone will help you master control over orgasm.

THE PATH TO ERECTION

As the penis engorges with blood, the testicles
enlarge and are drawn up closer to the body.

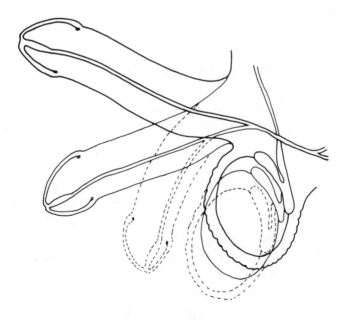

In the few seconds before orgasm, your nervous system relays a series of impulses to your spinal cord.

This begins a chain of events leading to the flow of semen—first from the testicles to the prostate, and then back down to the penis. Because the muscles involved are involuntary, their contractions generally don't reach your consciousness; you may not feel it happening, but you may get a kinesthetic awareness, a vague sensory perception.

Most men, however, can sense when the portion of the urethra located inside the prostate fills with prostatic fluid before the first ejaculatory contractions start. Once those contractions begin, at the moment called "ejaculatory inevitability," there's virtually nothing you can do to stop the process from reaching its foreordained conclusion.

What happens next is customarily called an orgasm. But there is an important distinction between ejaculation and orgasm.

Ejaculation is a physical fact: the bulbocavernosus muscle, extending back from the penis along the floor of the pelvis, contracts powerfully at rhythmic intervals of roughly eight-tenths of a second; the testicles rise up higher in the scrotal sac; and the penis expels semen—slightly less than one teaspoonful, or about three milliliters. The semen contains some 300 million sperm awash in discharges from the prostate gland and the seminal vesicles. The sphincter muscle surrounding the urethra where it enters the penis relaxes, and semen is ejected in intermittent waves, in the same rhythm as the contractions of the muscles on the floor of the pelvis and at the base of the penis.

But orgasm is not merely ejaculation. It's something

else entirely—a sensory experience akin to rapture, involving the whole body. Ejaculating quickly, for example after masturbating, isn't necessarily a particularly sensual event. But in orgasm you're swept away with a larger sense of release.

Orgasm is essentially a matter of perception, a constellation of physical and emotional sensations that transport you, however briefly, into an almost mystical state. Women relish witnessing the transformation in a man, and in doing whatever they can to enhance it:

Lori O., age 31:

Before my lover comes, there are obvious changes in his breathing and the way he moves and the noises he makes. But the general feeling —and maybe I just know it instead of feeling it—is of some kind of liquid, some kind of heat, and those intense and very deep movements that although brief feel better than anything that happened before. The experience is so intense, my pleasure in his pleasure. There seems to be a quality very different from a woman's orgasm. I did read in an article somewhere that the same things happen in a woman's body, but I sense a different quality anyway. I've talked to other women about it, and we all have this thing of opening our eyes at the last minute and watching, knowing that very small actions, like holding him tighter or digging your nails into his back, will make a big difference.

Elaine M., age 34:

When a man has an orgasm it's really wonderful. I love it when he cries out, maybe even swears. It also gives me a sense of power. It's a moment in a woman's life when she actually feels she has some control, which may be why sex became political for a lot of women in my generation. I think men now have more of a sense of needing to please women; it's their attempt to equalize something that's happened between us. Women aren't enslaved anymore, in the obvious ways that they used to be.

One of the great ironies of orgasm is that in order to have an erection you must be mentally and emotionally relaxed, but in the process of ejaculation your muscles have to tense. It's difficult to control the timing of an orgasm if you're anxious, or worrying about whether your partner is enjoying herself, or wondering whether your mother-in-law, sleeping in the room down the hall, is going to wake up and come knocking on the door. If you're under stress or don't have a peaceful environment for sexual pleasure, your body won't be free to experience all the feelings of arousal, and you will undoubtedly miss the cascade of sensations we call an orgasm. Timing is difficult for dozens of other individual reasons, but it is also the key to good sex. Think back on your own experience. When you were in sync with your partner, it made a difference. To good lovers timing becomes second nature. They make timing important and condition their responses so they don't have to give it a second thought.

The legendary pianist Claudio Arrau described in one sentence the secret of his lush concert technique: "The idea is to become one with the instrument." Arrau attributed his success to relaxing his body while not neglecting the intensity of the music: "One of the main problems in playing the piano is being able to stay physically relaxed in moments of great emotional tension."

The same may be said of sex. Intercourse is a kind of music, and the notes can be heard as your body transmits its nervous impulses. How much does your body hear? Recent research by Benjamin Graber at the University of Nebraska demonstrates that natural chemical transmitters in the brain affect the contractions of the pelvic musculature during orgasm, and thus the physical sensations of the sexual experience. We can turn those transmitters on or off depending on our mood; if we stifle our emotions, we'll stifle the physical sensations as well.

Hers

Not surprisingly, researchers who have patiently charted the sexual state have found that the physical changes leading to arousal and orgasm in women are similar to yours. When a woman is aroused, either by her thoughts or through physical stimulation, the clitoris engorges with blood and grows erect. The clitoris, unlike the penis, has no function other than sexual pleasure. Like the penis, though, the clitoris has a cluster of nerve endings. Both the head, called the glans, and the shaft are extraordinarily sensitive to the slightest touch. Some little girls learn to masturbate by rocking back and forth on the floor, a motion that stimulates the clitoris.

Most men, when asked how they think women masturbate, assume that a woman inserts her fingers into the vagina as a substitute penis; in fact, most women stimulate the area around the clitoris, rarely inserting fingers into the vagina. The vagina happens to be not nearly as richly supplied with sensory nerve endings as the clitoris. In fact, it is relatively insensitive to touch. But like many other hollows structures in the body, its nerves do respond to distension. Just as you can't actually feel food passing into or through your stomach, you can tell when you are full by the pleasant—or sometimes unpleasant—sensations of distension.

THE CLITORIS

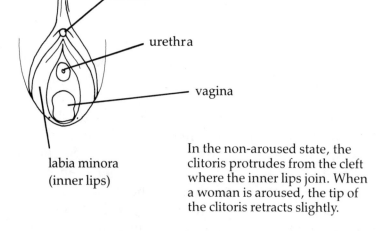

labia minora
(inner lips)

In the non-aroused state, the clitoris protrudes from the cleft where the inner lips join. When a woman is aroused, the tip of the clitoris retracts slightly.

A woman may enjoy having a penis inside her vagina for a variety of reasons. It's an object her muscles can contract against, but it's more than that. Her pleasure is that it's *your* penis—it's part of the man she's making love with. Even women who have located the G-spot would rather have it touched by the penis during intercourse than during masturbation:

Liza L., age 34:
> In masturbation I can get off myself, and I love orgasms. I prefer to have an orgasm every time I have sex, and I don't in intercourse. In fact, I very rarely do. In that sense, I guess masturbation's better. But obviously another person makes a difference, the feeling of another person makes it a lot nicer—somebody to cuddle up with and be with afterward. It's a man inside you, a penis, and when a man ejaculates, you can feel *that*. There's a little quiver, you can feel the liquid. And so intercourse is better.

As a woman becomes aroused, the veins in the vaginal walls dilate and, in conjunction with secretions from two small glands known as the Bartholin's glands, ooze fluid to lubricate the vagina—copiously in some women, less so in others. If a woman is not aroused, and her vagina is dry, penetration by the penis can be extraordinarily painful. But the presence of lubrication doesn't mean that a woman is ready to be penetrated; it's merely one of the first signs of arousal.

With increasing excitement, muscular contraction tugs on the vaginal walls; the vagina lengthens and dilates, preparing for penetration. The veins grow brighter with blood, and the outer lips pull back, exposing the vaginal opening. Women sometimes complain that men enter too quickly, not giving them enough time to reach the plateau phase before orgasm:

Barbara T., age 36
> I like a lot of foreplay. And when it's building up, I know it, my palms itch, they tingle, I feel it all over, and I really want it—meaning, well, I want to say, "Stick it in now." It's warm, it's hard, you can feel it against the uterus. There is a hole there, you know, and when he's inside it's tight and filled up to the end—well, it's filled, and I want it filled.

Women don't necessarily require extremely long periods of stimulation; in fact, they can masturbate themselves to orgasm almost as quickly as we can. But they need *steady* stimulation. Just as we do.

A woman's plateau phase is significantly different from yours. She can reach orgasm, descend to the plateau phase, and then have another orgasm within a matter of seconds. With all the emphasis on multiple orgasm, men worry more than ever about whether they're good lovers. The provider role no longer means merely making sure she has one orgasm; now she must have several, and you may feel you're solely responsible. But you're not. A woman who can have multiple orgasms will let you know how to help her, especially if you let her know you're willing to learn.

The best way to find out what your partner needs is not to try figuring it out. Instead, ask her. She can tell you how to touch her, how to stimulate her clitoris, where she likes to be touched. Every woman is different, and every time you make love is different. Sometimes you'll both need manual stimulation before intercourse; sometimes you won't. Some women like to have the outer lips of the vagina stroked; some women find oral sex more satisfying than anything you can do with your hands.

INTERCOURSE

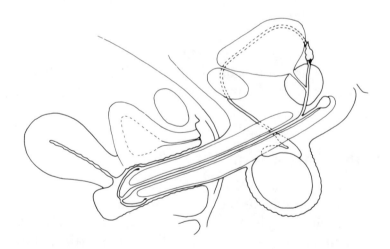

At penetration, the vaginal walls grip the penis. During thrusting, the inner lips are distended and tug at the hood of the clitoris, providing indirect stimulation.

Beth F., age 34:
> Men don't often ask what to do. I like every-
> thing that a man can do to stimulate me. Suck-
> ing my toes, whatever.

To reach orgasm during intercourse, most women
need clitoral stimulation. If this is true, many men
ask, then why aren't our bodies built to provide it? In
fact, they are. When the penis is moving back and
forth in the vagina, only rarely does it directly touch
the clitoris. But the smaller, or inner, lips of the vagina pull a fleshy cap of tissue, called the clitoral hood,
downward once you begin to thrust, thus giving indirect stimulation. Some positions are more effective than
others, and your partner may suggest them; a woman
on top, for example, with you on your back, can often
move to give herself direct clitoral stimulation. Chances
are she'll ask you what you need, too, which is far
better for both of you than guessing games.

Afterwards, and After Words

Once you have ejaculated, you enter what's called
the resolution phase. All the changes leading up to
orgasm are abruptly reversed. Your heartbeat and
breathing slow down, your testicles descend, and your
penis goes flaccid as the blood rushes out. The young-
er you are, the more slowly this will happen. How
quickly you become aroused again—the length of
what's called the refractory period—depends on your

age, your physical condition, and how tired you are.

Comedians have joked for years about men's habit of falling asleep immediately after they ejaculate. Women joke about it, too, but their feelings go deeper:

Melissa G., age 19:
I like a man to stay in me when he's done, keep that closeness, and let his penis just slide out in its due time.

Caroline F., age 26:
I'll tell you what's really key for me, what's really important: afterwards I want to be held. The biggest turnoff in the world is a man who just rolls over. I don't mind if he goes to sleep. A lot of men do go to sleep and that's nice, *if* he goes to sleep in my arms.

Our excuse for falling asleep has been that we're exhausted, it's over, we've done our job, now let us get some rest. The reason women are upset is right there in the language we use. We've done our job. When sex is work, it's no wonder we want to sleep when it's finished.

But if you habitually fall asleep seconds after you've ejaculated, you're missing one of the most enjoyable parts of intercourse. You and your partner have given each other pleasure, you're mellow and relaxed. And you're probably not feeling the usual bodily aches and pains. It has recently been discovered that sex is nature's very own aspirin; it releases the body's own pain-killing chemicals in the brain.

If you want to enhance your lovemaking technique, think about why you fall asleep. Are you feeling guilty about your own pleasure? Are you worried about what your partner might say if you gave her a chance to talk?

Try to stay awake the next time and see what happens. Rest your head on your partner's shoulder or on her chest and tell her how you feel. Or just put your arm around her and hug her. If sex is sharing, a form of communication, why let it end so quickly?

Hope N., age 28:
> I think for some men sex is something they just do—they start at the beginning and go through to the end. It's not something they do for fun, as sort of an overall, large endeavor. It's put the long part into the round part and then it's over. Those men who are very good lovers know that it's the whole environment and the whole interaction that really count.

The stages of sexual arousal—excitement, plateau, orgasm, and resolution—have been compared to climbing a mountain and plunging off the other side to a crash landing. This image may be descriptive of the physiologic sequence of buildup and letdown. But it's unfortunate in that it leaves so much unsaid. By attaching too much significance to the words we customarily use to describe the physical process of sex, we tend to blunt and obscure the emotional process, which doesn't have to have the same conclusion. We oughtn't become prisoners of our physiology or slaves to someone else's verbal analogies.

There is evidence that a counterpart to the well-publicized runner's high exists in sex: the sexual high. You have to learn to get there; you have to prepare your body through conditioning, and you have to open yourself to the experience. Your body—more specifically, chemicals in your brain known generally as endorphins—will take care of the rest. Attaining the sexual high can be as exquisite a sensual experience as the abandon you feel at the very moment of ejaculation; it can last longer than a mere crash landing and lead to a more fulfilling orgasm. The techniques for getting to the sexual high can be read but the experience is up to you—and your lover.

A Few Words About the Penis

Breathes there a man who has never worried about his penis? As one sex researcher remarked, Freud was wrong about women and penis envy; it's men who have the problem. A man catches a glimpse of other men in the locker room, he hears them talk about how they "wield the tool," and he compares. Either his isn't big enough or it doesn't get hard enough or it isn't ready when he wants it to perform.

Our worst tendency is to equate not only our sexuality but our entire being with our genitals, as in "He lost his manhood in the war," or, in the overheated prose of popular fiction, references to "his throbbing manhood." Enviously admiring the seducer of many women, we call him a "cocksman," and the sobriquet has a certain truth. If the thrill of conquest appeals to you more than intimacy, if quantity is more important than quality, then your cock *is* what makes you a man. In the words of an old joke, let's get something straight between us. Your penis doesn't make love, you do. And what determines your manhood is the quality of your life.

One reason we are obsessed with the penis as a symbol of manhood is our confusion over what it means to be a man. Although the roles of both sexes are in flux, women have an edge on us here. Women are reminded every month of their biological femininity. Men have no such biological marker. In a study of male and female roles, social psychologist Carol Tavris concluded that for a majority of men, masculinity is "a matter to be established against other males." For most men, Tavris discovered, masculinity has to be earned.

You can, however, keep your penis out of the battle. For one thing, most penises are roughly the same size. The average erect penis is six inches long and an inch and a half in diameter; some are bigger, of course, and some are smaller. But why measure? "I wouldn't care so much," you say, "if women didn't." Well, women don't.

In fact, an unusually long penis can be a liability. At the top of the vagina is the entrance to the uterus, a small doughnut-shaped structure called the cervix. Sperm pass through an opening in the center, no wider than the diameter of a pencil lead, on their way up through the uterus to the Fallopian tubes, where the egg is fertilized. During intercourse the vagina expands —balloons upward—so the cervix is out of the way.

But depending on the length of the penis and the position of intercourse, the cervix can be struck, and this is usually quite painful for the woman. As for width, the vagina contracts to accommodate any size. Indeed, according to a recent magazine survey, an exceptionally large penis gave men no decided advantage with most women. Any woman who measures your manhood by the size of your penis does you the same injustice too many men inflict on themselves.

CROSS-SECTION OF THE PENIS

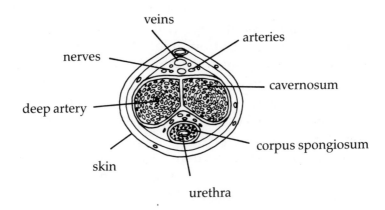

If This Is a Performance, Where's the Audience?

The other most common concern about the penis relates to its ability to get and stay erect. Often called performance anxiety, this is a by-product of the provider role in sex. If you don't get it up, she won't be happy. Or you'll wonder what's wrong with you. Without an erection, what else is there to do in bed?

Thinking about sex as a performance—whether that means always having an erection or always giving your partner an orgasm—is the surest way to deny yourself pleasure. Is there anyone among us who hasn't figuratively leapt for the scorecard? "Did you come?" "On a scale of one to ten, how was I?" A smile won't suffice; we demand a meter reading.

Here's a suggestion: throw your scorecard away. The very idea of performance implies work, and when making love becomes work, it stops being so much fun. Anxiety about getting an erection, in fact, often guarantees that you won't.

The old standard for success in bed used to be how many women you'd slept with or how many times you could ejaculate in one night. The new standard for many of us seems to be female applause, and applause by definition implies performance. If you're feeling anxious about audience response, try this: the next few times you make love, ask yourself who you're there for. If you regularly answer, "I'm here for her," then consider not making love until you can say, "I'm here for both of us," or even, "I'm here for me." This is not to imply that you should be there *only* for yourself —merely that you're entitled to consider your own pleasure as well as your partner's. And by pleasure this doesn't mean only the momentary sensations of ejaculation.

But granting yourself the right to pleasure is easier said than done. It requires that you allow yourself to relax. It means acknowledging that the boundaries of sex extend beyond chase and conquest. And it means you'll want to consider the possibility that your partner can give you pleasure. If you think this will detract from your technique, or if in your picture of the world women are completely selffocused and uninterested in your pleasure, you're in for a rewarding surprise.

Finetuning Your Body

Although your general physical condition affects your sexual experience in many ways, the strength of your abdominal and lower back muscles is especially important. If these muscles are flaccid and weak, you'll be limited in sheer physical stamina; you may find that extended lovemaking is more than your muscles can take. When your muscles are tense, you may experience a rush to ejaculation and miss many of the sensations of orgasm. If your trunk moves as a single unit and your pelvis can't "roll" with the rhythms of sex—a condition that the psychiatrist Wilhelm Reich called "frozen pelvis"—your sense of release and relaxation may feel less than satisfying even though you've ejaculated.

The PC: Exercising Aristotle's Muscle

One set of muscles is particularly important to the experience of intercourse and orgasm. These muscles support the pelvis and surround the sexual organs; although they contract throughout your pelvis when you ejaculate, you feel them most clearly in the Y-zone. They're part of a large structure known as the levators, and are called the coccygeus (pronounced cox-eh-*gee*-us), the iliococcygeus, and the pubococcygeus. The third is the thickest and most dominant, and so for convenience the whole group is referred to as the PC-muscle.

The muscle gets its name from what it's attached to—in front, the pubic bone (which lies just below where your pubic hair grows) and in back the coccyx, the bone at the bottom of your spine. It's a wide band that runs along both sides of your pelvis, passes below the bladder, and wraps under your rectum. When you have the urge to urinate and don't, or when you stop the flow of urine, you're contracting your PC muscle. Its importance to sexual response lies both in the support it provides within your pelvis and in the fact that its contractions transmit the physical sensations of orgasm to your brain.

Branches from the pudendal nerve serve the rear two-thirds of the PC muscle as well as the bulbocavernosus muscles at the root of the penis, which help expel the semen when you ejaculate. Increasing tension in these muscles (which occurs naturally as arousal builds) leads to the sensation of ejaculatory inevitability, that feeling of an orgasm about to occur. The sensation is initiated by nerve impulses carried along the pelvic nerve to the spinal cord and upward to the brain. A branch of the same nerve also serves the prostate in part of the reflex chain that sets off ejaculation. Equally significant are the sensations transmitted by contractions in the Y-zone, since these are part of that crucial sense of release that accompanies ejaculation.

TWO MAJOR MUSCLES OF THE MALE PELVIS

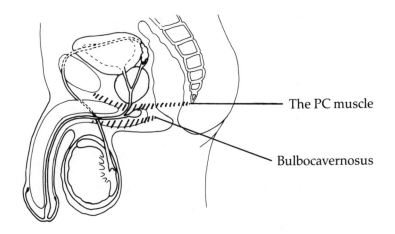

The PC muscle

Bulbocavernosus

The pubococcygeus is a broad muscular band that starts at the pubic bone and widens like a hammock at mid-body, where it is perforated by the rectum before attaching to the base of the spine (the coccyx). These two bony attachments designate the anatomical landmarks for which the muscle is named.

The bulbocavernosus, the other significant muscle, cradles the internal base of the penis. This muscle can be contracted at will, as is done to empty the urethra completely at the completion of urination.

As early as the 1920s physicians speculated that the PC muscle played a role in women's sexual response. In a popular sex manual published in 1926, a doctor named Theodore van der Velde suggested that exercising the pelvic muscles would enhance a woman's experience of orgasm. The medical profession paid little attention until the early 1940s when a surgeon and gynecologist named Arnold Kegel suggested PC-strengthening exercises to his patients as a cure for a variety of physical problems. Kegel theorized, too, that weak PC muscles accounted for the inability of some women to have orgasms.

Physicians and sex therapists have long since accepted the beneficial results of Kegel's exercises for women. But even in the fourth century B.C., Aristotle recognized the importance of the PC in men. "For it is impossible to emit semen without contracting the parts of the buttocks about the anus," Aristotle wrote. "The contraction forces out the moisture." Only recently, though, has there been medically documented evidence of the PC's effects on male sexual response. The latest discoveries reveal that the physical sensations of orgasm—our awareness of the contractions of the prostate, seminal vesicles, and other structures in the Y-zone—are intimately related to the PC-muscle.

This pattern of contractions is entirely different from any muscular response we can voluntarily produce. The strength of the contractions builds slowly until midway through the series. This might account for why some men feel a wave of sensations at the beginning of orgasm and then a "peak"—a more intense spreading of sensation throughout the entire pelvic region.

You can build up your biceps at a gym, strengthen your legs by jogging; you'll look better and probably feel sexier. But unlike our external muscles, the PC muscle gets no natural exercise, except perhaps at the end of urination. Kegel speculated that the PC might, in fact, be vestigial—having once served, in the course of evolution, to wag the human tail, then fallen into disuse. But the muscle can be consciously strengthened by means of simple exercises requiring very little time.

You can tell what condition your PC muscle is in by testing its tone and strengthen yourself. Tone means the degree of resistance a muscle offers to pressure. Strength means your muscle's ability to contract against opposition.

To find your PC muscle, lie down on your back and tighten the muscle you would tighten to hold back the flow of urine. If your abdominal and thigh muscles move, you're tensing the wrong muscle, try again. You should be able to feel the muscle tighten midway up your rectum.

To check the muscle's tone, insert a finger about two inches into your rectum. (You may want to use a lubricant like K-Y jelly, which is what your doctor uses during a rectal exam.) Tense the muscle to clamp it around your finger; if it tightens, you'll know you've found the right spot. Then push downward toward the pelvis. A muscle with good tone will provide relatively firm resistance. To test your PC-muscle's strength, try what's called the "washcloth trick." Hang a washcloth or a small hand towel over your erect penis. By tightening and releasing your PC muscle, you should be able to move the washcloth up and down. This is also a good exercise for the muscle. (Since you may feel foolish doing this, you should probably try it privately.) Even if your PC-muscle's tone and strength could be improved, now that you know where this muscle is you should be able to notice it contracting the next time you have intercourse.

Strengthening your PC-muscle is only a matter of using it by deliberately giving it some exercise. All you have to do is contract the muscle, hold the contraction for ten seconds or so, then relax. You can do it standing on line at the movies, while waiting for the light to change when you're driving, or when you're on the phone and you've been put on "hold." Try to repeat the exercise two or three times a day. Within five or six weeks you should notice a difference in the quality of your orgasms—more awareness of your rising level of arousal, a clearer sense of when you're nearing ejaculation, and more forceful ejaculation, with increased sensation throughout your pelvis.

Exercises for the Erogenous Zone

These seven floor exercises for pelvic strength and lower back flexibility will specifically fine-tune areas of your body that are central to the act of intercourse. They can be done in about eight to ten minutes a day and should be repeated three to five times a week. Pay particular attention to the breathing sequences and follow the instructions closely. Each should be begun as a set of five (five repetitions of the specific exercise). You'll notice improved flexibility and strength within the first two weeks. You'll also experience heightened awareness of your own sensuality and a sense of control over your body during lovemaking. The maximum number of repetitions is twenty; there is little benefit to be gained beyond that level. The important thing is to continue. As with all exercises there is a training effect when they are done regularly. The level of conditioning begins to taper off gradually within three days of ending any exercise regimen.

1. Pelvic Tilt

FOCUS: The abdomen, buttocks, hamstrings, inner thighs. The PC-muscle can also be enlisted here if you consciously constrict the urethra and anus through the upward tilting motion. This exercise, a slow, sustained contraction, uses the hip joint as an axis to give flexibility to the normally curved lumbar (mid) section of the spine.

STARTING POSITION: Lying flat on your back on an exercise mat or carpeted floor, arms extended along your sides, palms down. Your knees should be raised to form approximately a 90-degree angle. Your feet should be flat on the floor.

THE EXERCISE: Concentrate on an imaginary line running through your body from side to side between the center points of your hips. Keep your spine as flat against the floor as possible. Relax. Inhale gently and, with a slow upward rolling motion, raise your lower abdomen, aiming your genitals at a spot directly overhead. Do this as a slow steady upward thrust, exhaling steadily through a count of four as you extend your lower abdomen up without allowing your lower back to raise off the floor. The midsection of your spine should remain flush against the floor as you tighten your buttocks and thrust upward. Hold at the top for a count of three, and then, inhaling through a count of four, return slowly to the starting position.

MINIMUM REPETITIONS: 5

MAXIMUM REPETITIONS: 4 sets of 5 complete sequences

2. Pelvic Tilt (Legs Extended)

FOCUS: This is an exercise for hip and lumbar spinal mobility. Although it is similar to the Pelvic Tilt, the focus is slightly less on the buttocks and more directly on the lower abdominal cavity. Most exercises for the abdomen disproportionately affect the upper portion. This one directly affects the tissues of the lower abdomen that are so important in intercourse.

STARTING POSITION: Flat on your back, arms extended along your sides, palms down. Legs fully extended on the floor.

THE EXERCISE: Keep your buttocks, legs, and heels as flat on the floor as possible. Contract your abdomen and thrust your pubic area (lower abdomen) toward an imagined point on the ceiling directly above your eyes, while exhaling to a slow count of four. Hold at the top for a count of three. Then return slowly through a count of four to your starting position with a sustained, conscious inhale.

MINIMUM REPETITIONS: 5

MAXIMUM REPETITIONS: 5

3. Drawbridge Movement

FOCUS: The buttocks, hamstrings, lower abdomen, front of the thighs, and the hip-flexor group. During this exercise you experience a hyperextension of the lower back. As you raise to the top, you'll feel increased tension in your hamstrings from the midpoint of the thighs into the buttocks.

STARTING POSITION: Flat on your back, arms extended along your sides, palms down. Knees bent at approximately a 90 degree angle. Feet flat on the floor.

THE EXERCISE: The first part of this exercise is a repetition of the Pelvic Tilt. Inhale, then roll and thrust your pubic area as high as you can with your midspine against the floor. Then continue thrusting up, aided by a little pressure from the palms of your hands against the floor. Allow your buttocks, and then your lower back and the midspine area to raise up, in an even flowing sequence, pulled by your lower abdomen, as you transfer your weight to your shoulders. Sustain a slow exhale to the count of four as you raise up. Hold at the top for a count of three, and then roll down, again exhaling through a count fo four.

MINIMUM REPETITIONS: 5

MAXIMUM REPETITIONS: 4 sets of 5 complete sequences

4. Pelvic Tilt, Side to Side

FOCUS: This exercise is designed to develop vertical flexibility of the pelvis and hips. By tilting the pelvis as far down to the left and to the right as it can go, you are exercising the muscles of the hip flexor and those in the deep front abdominal wall. You're also using the oblique muscles of the abdominal cavity.

STARTING POSITION: Flat on your back, arms extended along your side, palms down, legs extended.

THE EXERCISE: Exhaling through a count of two, tilt the right side of your pelvis by extending your right leg farther, pressing from the hip joint toward the sole of your foot, until your right foot extends an inch or two beyond your left. Hold for one count and return to the starting position, inhaling through a count of two. Hold for one count and repeat the motion on your left side, tilting the pelvis toward your left foot so that it extends beyond the right. Return again to the starting position and hold for one count before repeating the sequence. As you gain flexibility, you'll find that each foot can be extended three to four inches beyond the other at the maximum extension.

MINIMUM REPETITIONS: 5 complete sequences, counting extended-right-return-left-extended-return as a single sequence

MAXIMUM REPETITIONS: 4 sets of 5 complete sequences

5. Leg Lifts

FOCUS: Hip flexors, lower abdomen, buttocks, pelvis, thighs.

STARTING POSITION: Flat on your back, with knees sharply bent, feet flat on the floor.

THE EXERCISE: Grip each leg just below the kneecap and draw your knees up toward your chest. Keep your upper spine and head flat on the floor. Concentrate on the muscles of your lower abdomen as you draw up through a count of four, exhaling throughout the move. Hold for a count of two, and then, inhaling through a count of four, slowly return to the starting position. Hold for a count of two before repeating the exercise.

MINIMUM REPETITIONS: 5

MAXIMUM REPETITIONS: 4 sets of 5

VARIATIONS: After a week or two of doing the exercise with your head against the floor, try raising your head as you bring your knees to your chest. As you gain additional flexibility, the exercise can be done with arms extended out from your sides, using only the muscles of your lower abdomen and hip flexors for power. The maximum number of repetitions remains 20.

6. Leg Crosses

FOCUS: Pelvis, inner thighs, hip flexors.

STARTING POSITION: Flat on your back, arms outstretched from your sides, palms up. Knees bent at approximately a 90-degree angle, feet flat on the floor.

THE EXERCISE: Cross your left leg over your right leg and rest the lower calf of the crossing left leg at a point on your upper right thigh just below the kneecap. Using the weight of your left leg, press the right leg toward the right. Concentrate on keeping your shoulders, spine, and lower back as firmly on the floor as possible. As you press, exhale slowly through a count of four. Hold at your most extended position for two counts. Then, maintaining resistance with both legs, inhale slowly and deeply through a count of four as you return to the starting position.Hold for a count of two before repeating the exercise, exhaling again as you move the right leg out to the right. Repeat this five times and then alter your leg positions, placing the right leg over the left.

MINIMUM REPETITIONS: 5 to the right, 5 to the left

MAXIMUM REPETITIONS: 4 sets each of 5 to the right, 5 to the left

7. Seated Leg Pulls

FOCUS: Buttocks, inner thighs, lower abdomen, lower spinal flexibility.

STARTING POSITION: Sitting, as erect as possible, legs outstretched. Hands to the sides and slightly to the rear, palms flat against the floor. Your fingers should be pointing away from your body. Your weight is supported by your arms and hands.

THE EXERCISE: Cross your left leg, bent at the knee, over your extended right leg. Put your left foot firmly on the floor at least as close to your body as the right knee. Then lean slightly into the crossing leg and pull it up a bit tighter, so that your foot is right next to or slightly above the knee. Take hold of your left leg along the ankle with your right hand, supporing your weight with your left arm. Sit as erect as possible. Exhale through a count of four as you gently pull the leg toward your chest. At the same time rotate your shoulders and head to the left. (This seems to stretch the buttocks.) Hold for a count of two, and then inhale through a count of four. Return to the starting position. Repeat this a minimum of five times before reversing leg positions and repeating the exercise.

MINIMUM REPETITIONS: 5 left over right, 5 right over left

MAXIMUM REPETITIONS: 4 sets each of 5 to the right and 5 to the left

General Conditioning

The real measure of how much and what kind of general exercise you need has to be the one you take yourself. How do you look and feel? If you're easily winded, and less than firm and toned-looking, you're out of shape—and you know it. *Admitting* that you know it is the part that comes hard. But admit it you must, because you need exercise. Without it you become mentally slushy, physically flabby, and more susceptible to fatigue and illness.

Find a general exercise routine that you can enjoy and look forward to. That way you're more likely to stick with it—for life.

If you begin a new form of general exercise, put yourself in the hands of a skilled instructor. He'll teach you the right way to breathe, how to pay attention to your body, how to have the right mental attitude about what you're doing.

If time and bad habits have taken their toll on your physical condition, reverse the process. Now, no matter what your age. You can have a healthy, beautiful and sensual body.

The Delay Reflex

Here are the facts: sex research shows that any man can learn to control the timing of his orgasm. Moreover, you can enable yourself to maintain high levels of sexual arousal without ejaculating by training the delay reflex.

All reflexes in the body work essentially the same way. Impulses in one or more nerves are triggered by some internal or external stimulus. The impulse then travels along the nerve path to the spinal cord, where other nerves are stimulated to produce a muscular response. When a physician taps your knee and your leg jerks, that is a reflex. You do not have to consciously "tell" your leg to jerk. It happens involuntarily. There are thousands of such automatic responses in the body, most of which we are not aware of at all, particularly those that occur entirely internally, such as those that take place during arousal.

Arousal reflexes, for example, move sperm from the testes to the ejaculatory ducts and prepare the seminal vesicles, the prostate, and other glands for ejaculation. These reflexes are controlled by the autonomic nervous system via nerve fibers that leave the spinal cord to enter nearby junctions called ganglia. From the ganglia they extend to involuntary muscles, such as those that open blood vessels in the penis to permit erection, or to glandular cells, such as those that release prostatic fluid.

The existence of an arousal reflex was known as far back as 1917. Research on soldiers who suffered spinal cord injuries, published in the journal *Brain*, showed that a light touch to the pelvis, totally devoid of sexual innuendo, could produce erection and sometimes ejaculation.

In normal circumstances arousal reflexes, as well as many other kinds of reflexes, are accompanied by sensations that do reach consciousness. Or they may be initiated by conscious thoughts alone. Fantasizing about sex can produce an erection as effectively as the touch of your lover at the beginning of foreplay. But the stimulus of touch alone is not sufficient for arousal. If it were, you'd have an erection every time you touched your penis. The arousal reflex does not take place in a vacuum. You have to be ready for sex or at least mentally receptive. If you're tense, anxious, or distressed, arousal will be delayed or blocked entirely. So your brain plays a role—a critical one at that—in arousal and in initiating the reflexes that prepare your body for sex and orgasm.

Arousal reflexes—again like many other kinds of reflexes —can be conditioned by experience. The Russian physiologist Ivan Pavlov demonstrated the conditioning process in a famous series of experiments on dogs. He knew that dogs salivate when they smell food, and that salivation is a reflex. To prove that the reflex could be conditioned or altered to respond to stimuli other than food, he rang a bell at feeding time. The dogs quickly learned to associate the ringing bell with food, and Pavlov found that his research animals would salivate at the sound of the bell alone, without any food present.

The formation of certain habits may rely on the imposition of mental control over these reflexes. When we exercise control over certain reflexes over a period of time, we are in effect conditioning them. Infants, for example, have little or no control over urination. It is simply a reflex that is initiated when the bladder distends to a certain point. But as they become toilet-trained, they gain control over the bladder reflex and can consciously delay it; it becomes a conditioned reflex.

Reflexes involved in orgasm are believed by most sex researchers to be subject to conditioning. Early experimenting with sex conditions most men to ejaculate quickly when aroused by sexual stimuli. But this conditioning can be easily reversed by reconditioning.

The process of reflex retraining entails a very simple exercise in awareness that soon becomes second nature. At the beginning you'll have to exercise some conscious control. In effect, you'll be conditioning your delay reflex, but the process is entirely pleasant, and the sensations can open the door to exquisite sexual feelings inside your body that you may not have experienced as fully before.

As arousal builds toward ejaculation, the sensation of sperm filling the tubular vas deferens, which lead upwards from the testicles, and of ducts filling with the fluid components of semen, can get lost in the head-long rush to ejaculation. But if you are aware of what your body is doing, if you decide to feel what is happening inch by inch, stage by stage, you'll have no trouble experiencing these sensations. You may not be able to consciously distinguish each stage—hardly anyone is—but you'll notice subtly pleasant changes in the ducts that carry sperm and seminal fluid and in the tension of muscles that extend along the Y-zone.

These sensations are never as fully felt—not as satisfying—as ejaculation. They do not come in regular waves, as ejaculation does. But there are irregular contractions that can be sensed in the muscles along the Y-zone. These are not as powerful as ejaculatory contractions; nonetheless, they do contribute to building up the volume of semen that will eventually be ejaculated. The longer ejaculation can be delayed by the exercise of control over the ejaculatory reflex, the more semen will be conducted to the ejaculatory ducts, and the more sustained the orgasm will be as a result.

Ejaculation is the final reflex in the cascade of arousal reflexes. It takes place in two more or less distinct phases, emission and ejaculatory. As you become more aware of sensations in your Y-zone, you'll be better at distinguishing between them. The emission phase, the most important to get to know in conditioning the delay reflex, involves contractions of muscles and glands, including the prostate and the seminal vesicles, which are under the control of autonomic fibers in the pelvic nerve. These contractions can be sensed internally with practice, but they are most readily apparent to inquiring fingertips placed on the Y-zone. It is here, along the sensitive skin between the scrotum and anus, that the superficial muscles of the Y-zone, particularly the bulbocavernosus muscle, can be felt. The deeper PC muscle is not accessible to the touch, but its contractions can be sensed. The portion of the PC muscle closest to the pubic bone is served by the pelvic nerve, while the portion farther back is served by the pudendal nerve. The pudendal nerve supplies the bulk of the sensory fibers (fibers, in this case, that can be stimulated by touch) that make the glans of the penis, and the skin of the Y-zone, so highly sensitive during arousal that they are known as erogenous zones.

Although the various muscles of the Y-zone have somewhat distinct roles in erection and ejaculation, they function at other times as a single mass that supports all the structures in the pelvis, including the bladder, the rectum, and the prostate, among others.

During the emission phase of the ejaculatory reflex, when the genital structures have moved just beyond the "on the mark" stage to the "get set" position, the pelvic nerve reflex initiates the sensations of ejaculatory inevitability. This is the hallmark of emission. It lasts only a few seconds and involves contractions of the prostate and other associated glands, along with irregular contractions of the PC muscle that can be vaguely sensed. This is the now-or-never time for the delay reflex. A second or two more, and ejaculation is triggered.

When you are first experimenting with these sensations, don't be disappointed at not being able to stop before ejaculation. It takes a half dozen or so tries, sometimes more. Soon enough, though, you'll recognize the preliminary sensations of inevitability, and once you do, you'll be able to take charge and control the outcome without mentally removing yourself from what's going on.

Once you've become familiar with the sensations in the Y-zone leading up to your own emission phase, you can learn to use pressure on the PG-point. This technique is extremely helpful in mastering control over the timing of ejaculation. Your individual PG-point, the spot on your Y-zone that is most sensitive to touch, may be closer to the scrotum or the anus depending on individual variability, but for most men it is closer to the scrotum. The sensory fibers near the surface of the skin at the PG-point come from the pudendal nerve, the same nerve that supplies the top of the penis with sensory fibers and the bulk of the PC muscle with autonomic fibers.

Light, feathery touching at this spot is invariably stimulating during intercourse, but harder pressure upward into the pelvis at the PG-point produces slight discomfort. Such pressure can be used to briefly disengage arousal by blocking reflex activity that would otherwise ready the prostate for emission. Release of pressure at the PG-point, and resumption of other sexual stimuli, especially the sensations produced by moving the penis in the vagina, will reestablish arousal. Depending on your desire and your partner's, you may choose to proceed to orgasm.

The ejaculatory phase of the ejaculatory reflex follows the emission phase. Semen is propelled through the urethra by strong contractions of the PC and bulbocavernosus muscles as an inevitable consequence of the pudendal reflex.

Why Orgasm Sneaks Up on You

We're primed to ejaculate quickly by both nature and nurture—by biology, that is, and by the lessons we learned growing up. Nature's role is easy to understand. Among the jobs we're built for is reproducing the species, a task nature would prefer us to accomplish as efficiently and quickly as possible. The effect of nature's role is one we have all experienced: when the Y-zone meets the G-spot, we feel we have no control, that the penis has a mind of its own.

But nurture, and particularly our early sexual experiences, may play an even larger role in determining how quickly we ejaculate. "The sexual taboo and the antisexual ideology of our society," writes Dr. John Money of Baltimore's Johns Hopkins Hospital, "is nowhere stronger than with respect to the developmental sexuality of children." Many of us first encounter the mysteries of intercourse in situations in which we are tense, highly excited, and anxious to explore uncharted territory as fast as possible. We tend to ejaculate quickly out of nervousness, partly because we are afraid of being discovered, and also because when we're young, our sexual responses are at their peak. Or we thrust a few frenzied times, attempt to hold back, and then frantically withdraw, afraid of an unwanted pregnancy. These early experiences are major milestones in our lives, and as we grow older the pattern we learned as adolescents repeats itself. It's what behavioral psychologists call a conditioned response, and what the rest of us call a habit. Sometimes, too, we equate coming quickly with our idea of manhood; one test of "a real man" is his speed to orgasm.

But adolescent habits can't entirely account for the urge to rapid ejaculation. A more important factor is that we don't listen to our bodies during intercourse. We miss our own crescendo of sexual excitement. New research done at the University of Minnesota shows that most men can't tell precisely when an orgasm begins; using a pressurized probe inside the rectum, doctors have discovered that some men don't notice obvious physiological signs, such as contractions of the pelvic muscles, until as long as seven or eight seconds after the process has started.

Why are we so insensitive to ourselves, to both our bodies and our feelings? Anxiety is perhaps our greatest enemy. If you're worried about your performance, if you're not confident that your partner cares for you, if you think your body isn't beautiful, all these doubts prevent you from immersing yourself in the pleasure of sex. Many of us labor under exaggerated ideas of what to expect from ourselves during sex, not the least being that a man is always ready—able to get an erection at any moment. Combined with the biological signals that have been bred into men by evolution, it's no wonder you give in to the natural urge to ejaculate. If you're both anxious and highly aroused, timing an orgasm is well nigh impossible. This is why we often ejaculate quickly after a period of abstinence or when we're making love for the first time with a new partner.

If you once conditioned your reflexes to ejaculate at top speed, you can now recondition them. But it's not simply a question of physiology, of learning techniques to delay orgasm. It's learning to change how you experience sex. A common complaint of women is that during intercourse men are often absent; their minds are elsewhere. By staying in touch with both the emotional and physical feelings of intercourse, you can retrain both the body and the mind—or rather, you can bring them together.

INSIDE VIEW OF THE TESTICLE

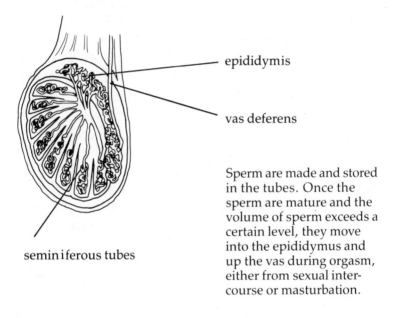

epididymis

vas deferens

seminiferous tubes

Sperm are made and stored in the tubes. Once the sperm are mature and the volume of sperm exceeds a certain level, they move into the epididymus and up the vas during orgasm, either from sexual intercourse or masturbation.

Breathing

We've been breathing since birth. What's there to learn? And we associate being breathless with making love—the stereotypical clichés are about panting, gasping, coming up for air. Isn't that part of what it's all about—doing what comes naturally? If, however, we were doing what comes naturally we'd be breathing as babies do—through the nose, and very deeply. Mouth breathing and chest breathing are an adaptive response. The short breaths of chest breathing begin only when an infant begins socializing and moves out of the crib. And deep breathing, breathing naturally, becomes something that many of us have to relearn.

Specific breathing techniques are taught for many functions that require physical and mental coordination. Tennis: inhale deeply during your backstroke and exhale completely as you strike and hit through the ball. Relieve stress: take deep breaths—inhale slowly, exhale slowly and evenly. Jogging: breathe deeply in an even steady rhythm timed to the cadence of your pace. Sprinting: suck the air in as deeply as possible; begin exhaling as you spring from the starting blocks and continue to exhale as you exert yourself throughout an entire hundred meter race. And musicians, singers, public speakers, dancers, swimmers, and weight lifters, to name but a few, profit from training in deep breathing, designed to maximize their physical and emotional effectiveness in their own disciplines.

Although these techniques are learned actions, they do become "natural" to the people who utilize them. Once a person has been trained, the pattern becomes unconscious except to the degree that an individual uses a heightened awareness of the breathing rhythm to focus more intensely upon the moment at hand. And by learning and using very specific and simple deep breathing techniques, you can heighten the sensuality, pleasure, and excitation of intercourse.

One of the elements of the great comfort between a man and a woman, between two lovers in bed, both during and after lovemaking is the metronomic effect, on each, of the other's breathing pattern. Clearly, part of the difficulty in sleeping experienced by many people who separate for periods of time, interrupting or ending long-standing relationships, is the absence of a partner's particular pattern of breathing and movement and undulation on the bed. In a very real sense the breathing pattern and rhythm are a direct form of communication between partners and within one's self.

The act of intercourse, sharing and being close, is perhaps the most unique and intimate experience a man and a woman can share, and deep rhythm breathing is important in allowing the body and mind to blend and flow with the moments. Many men, however, feel a need to be physically tense to avoid conveying false impressions through body language —language that they've heard about and experienced in lovemaking. If you relax, it means to your partner that you've had an orgasm, or that something went wrong, or that the partner is supposed to start doing something. The body language that many people have become locked into says that intercourse has to be a steady progression. So, some men have "learned" not to allow themselves to relax.

The simple fact is that you don't have to be in a state of constant tension during intercourse. Your body does not have to be rigid. You can relax and still maintain an erection. And, instead of losing enjoyment or forfeiting any pleasure, you can emotionally and physically experience the moment even more intensely. Lovemaking doesn't have to be a steady progression. You can and should explore and experience ways to have fun with your own body while giving pleasure. And you and your partner have to be there to enjoy it. That's where breathing technique can make a difference.

There's an old story about the ship's captain who before going to the bridge of his ship each day would open a safe in his cabin and study a small scrap of paper. After his death which ended a long career at sea, his first mate forced open the safe to glimpse the captain's secret. Printed carefully across the paper were these words "Port means left; starboard means right." A deep breathing technique that can heighten the sensuality of intercourse can be condensed as neatly: inhale deeply while thrusting, exhale fully when drawing back.

Of course there's more to it. Inhaling during the forward movement of the pelvis means that the diaphragm contracts, relaxing the muscles of the lower abdomen and the PC muscle, and slowing the direct progression to orgasm. Exhaling fully while drawing back causes a less than maximum constriction of the same muscle groups, since the muscle presure is contained. As this can delay orgasm, the reverse—exhaling fully when thrusting, inhaling deeply when drawing back —can and does lead in a direct line to orgasm. Perhaps the easiest way to experience the differences in these two breathing patterns is to stand with your back against a wall. With a movement similar to the Pelvic Thrust exercise on page 72, swing foreward as in intercourse, keeping your back and legs close to the wall, while inhaling deeply—and draw back while exhaling fully. Repeat this a few times and then change the inhale-exhale movement count, first slowing down the rhythm and then speeding up the sequenced deep breathing.

This is the reverse of the deep breathing exercise techniques that have become familiar to many through Nautilus training and/or Universal weight training. The goal of such anaerobic exercises is to maximize muscular tension. Weight exercises call for a pattern of exhaling during the specific periods of muscle stress (thrusting, pushing, straining) and inhaling during the moments still in motion of minimal stress or regrouping. But not surprisingly, intercourse is not a weight-training exercise. During intercourse, exhaling during the movement of maximum action, the thrust, tenses the PC-muscle and the muscles of the lower abdomen, and if you're in a rush to orgasm, this helps you get there quickly. To experience this, try reversing the standing exercise sequence to the Nautilus pattern. Exhale while moving forward, inhale while drawing back. The tension throughout the pelvic area will be heightened.

You can match your breathing with the way you want your body to work. Sexual tension is muscular. The sexual curve ascends as we become more sexually aroused, and our muscles become more tense. This means they are tighter, more constricted. And muscles require more oxygen when they are constricted. By filling our muscles with more oxygen—through deep abdominal breathing, minimizing the stress on the PC and lower abdominal muscles—we can delay or postpone the climax. Conversely, by reversing the breathing sequence or by lessening oxygen intake through chest breathing or holding one's breath, an oxygen debt is created that hurries one toward orgasm.

For most of us, reaching orgasm in a direct line has not been the problem. Inhaling deeply during the thrust, however, and exhaling during withdrawal, leaves the PC muscle group relatively relaxed during the muscular stress phase and yet gives you the oxygen needed to maintain an active and fully involved state of arousal.

The Distancing Maneuver

Most of us do exercise some control over the timing of orgasm in intercourse, even if we're not always aware of how we do it. The method men resort to most often is mentally stepping away from their bodies—the distancing maneuver. Woody Allen illustrated this idea with both pathos and humor in *Annie Hall*. In bed with Diane Keaton, he tells her she doesn't seem involved. And Woody's right; she isn't. A transparent version of her sits, bored, watching from a nearby chair. Chances are you've done something similar for different reasons—you've thought about your budget or transferred your attention to what's going on outside the bedroom window, in an effort to avoid reaching orgasm. This is the emotional equivalent of a cold shower, a technique with which men have long been familiar. In the East Indies it was once common practice for men to plunge their hands into ice water to forestall orgasm.

Another way you may have tried to decrease your speed toward orgasm is by changing the pace and intensity of your thrusts, or by shifting position. You consciously try to diminish your level of arousal by physically breaking the rhythm.

These methods work, of course, but have a decided disadvantage. While you're thinking of other things or mechanically slowing down, you're also disengaging from the intimacy of the sexual act. The word intimacy comes from the Latin *intimus*, meaning "innermost." But it is precisely our innermost feelings we neglect when we consciously detach ourselves from lovemaking. There is a better alternative: making love with both sides of your brain. This means experiencing the physical and emotional feelings of sex at the same time.

But isn't it difficult, you might ask, to stay engaged in the pleasure of sex when we're also *thinking* about sex? Doesn't giving ourselves over to sensuality mean emptying our minds, concentrating on sensations? No, because your mind is registering the sensations. When you make love with both sides of your brain, you can feel sensual—attuned to your body; sexual—attuned to your desire for physical intimacy; and emotional —attuned to your loving feelings for your partner.

Having a Choice

Not every sexual experience has to last for hours. Sometimes we want to go on forever, and sometimes we're happy with a "quickie." Both can be fine, for men *and* women, as can everything in between. What's not so wonderful is having no choice.

Much has been made lately of a phenomenon called premature ejaculation. Nobody seems exactly sure what it is, but medical awareness of the idea has been around for a long time. In 1899 the aforementioned Dr. Lewis spoke of a husband who would arrive home "from the club at midnight and find his wife in bed and half asleep. Erection is speedily followed by intromission, and often before the wife is fully awake, the orgasm has occurred." In 1910 the Hungarian sexologist Ferenczi pointed out that "the whole male sex suffer from precocious ejaculation."

Sex researchers now define premature ejaculation

as meaning anything from ejaculating before intercourse begins to not being able to last long enough to please your partner at least half the time. But what does "long enough" mean? In a loving relationship, with two people enjoying each other's sexuality, there is no right or wrong way to have intercourse. Lasting long enough means, simply, whatever you and your partner think it means. Depending on her mood and yours, ten minutes may be too long, half an hour not long enough. The best definition of premature ejaculation, then, may be reaching orgasm before you're ready.

Thirty-five years ago Alfred Kinsey reported that three-quarters of all men ejaculated within two minutes of beginning intercourse. According to current studies, the figure for most men, even exercising some control, is between six and eight minutes. Because these numbers are often based on self-reporting —dependent, that is, on what men tell researchers— they have to be taken with at least a grain or two of salt. But it's a safe assumption that for most of us, exercising no control at all, four to six minutes is the outside limit.

We feel a lot of pressure—from ourselves, mostly— to delay orgasm. Conventional wisdom tells us that the longer we last, the more we'll satisfy our partners. Because women take somewhat longer to reach orgasm during intercourse, this argument goes, we should want to maintain "staying power." But as we know now, not all women reach orgasm during intercourse, and those who do certainly don't do it every time. Ignorance about women's sexual enjoyment leads some men to "slam" as hard as possible for as long as possible, assuming their partner will

scream in ecstasy and award the Greatest Lover tro-
phy with eyes full of tears and gratitude. The fact is
that this approach will nearly always make your partner physically uncomfortable, bored, or both.

But regardless of whether your partner reaches orgasm during intercourse, she may enjoy the act for its
own sake— for the feelings of intimacy it brings. And
she can tell you how to help her stay in a relatively
high state of arousal. Finding out what your partner
enjoys—how long she would like intercourse to last
on a given occasion, the kind of stimulation she needs
—goes a long way toward enhancing your lovemaking technique. Equally important, it helps you become
a sexual partner, not a performer.

You, too, may find that intercourse provides its own
satisfactions separate from orgasm, and so increasing
your ejaculatory control can heighten your own
pleasure. Think, for example, of swirling a sip of fine
wine across your tongue before swallowing. You savor
the taste, luxuriate in the delicate flavor. The same
can be said for sexual arousal. For many men, six or
seven minutes isn't sufficient to reach a complete
orgasm; you may ejaculate but not feel the sensations
throughout your body. In fact, physicians at the University of Nebraska have discovered the presence of
chemicals that control the transmission of impulses in
what scientists call the "pleasure sites" of the brain;
these act either to speed up or to slow down the onset
of contractions leading to orgasm. What you're feeling during intercourse is partly responsible for releasing or suppressing those chemicals and so affects the
intensity of your orgasm.

There is one final and somewhat ironic reason

why learning ejaculatory control will enhance both your lovemaking technique and your pleasure. Many men understand that their fear of losing control in sex, of succumbing to the rush of physical and emotional feelings, inhibits their enjoyment. Outside the bedroom we sometimes have no choice; we control our tempers or our urges to buy expensive household gadgets. And so we're stymied when we'd like to let go during sex; we feel overwhelmed, even frightened. The best cure for fear of losing control is gaining control. Once you realize that you can control the timing of your orgasm, you may find the freedom to enjoy all the sensations that precede it.

Male Multiple Orgasm: Does It Exist?

Of all the persistent sexual myths, one of the most powerful is that men are more sexual than women. This notion didn't begin to die until we realized that women can have multiple orgasms, series of sexual peaks that often last for more than a full minute, while men's orgasms seem to be over in a matter of seconds.

Men can have multiple ejaculations, although the number of times we can come in one afternoon or evening decreases as we get older. But there is another kind of male multiple orgasm, once we accept the idea that orgasm is not identical to ejaculation. Sex researchers have monitored the physiological changes leading to ejaculation. What they've discovered is that in the plateau phase many men can reach the brink of ejaculation, hold back, and still experience virtually all of the changes accompanying orgasm —contractions of the pelvic muscles, increased heart rate, even the anal contractions that you feel to one degree or another, depending on the condition of your PC muscle. The experience won't be the same as a woman's multiple orgasm but has its own rewards.

There's no point, however, in setting a goal—"I want to experience the sensations of orgasm four times and then come." The physiology of sex can be separated from the emotions in a laboratory, but when you do that to yourself you separate yourself from the pleasure of the moment. Aiming for the sensation of multiple orgasms every time can be as self-defeating as aiming for simultaneous orgasm or orgasm when the clock chimes midnight. The possibility of male multiple orgasms is mentioned because on any given night you and your partner may both be in the mood for extended lovemaking. Reaching the brink and retreating is one way to enhance both your technique and your pleasure.

Staying with the Feeling

In our culture—Western, late twentieth century—sex has become centered on objects, not people. Our pornography, for example, only rarely offers sensuality or humor. Particularly for men, making love takes place between a penis and a vagina. All too often we define sexual arousal solely by the hardness and duration of an erection.

The truth is simple but difficult for many of us to understand. When we were told "Big boys don't cry," not only did we learn not to cry, we learned to stifle a whole range of emotions—what psychologists call "affective states." In plain language, we literally ignore our own feelings. Or, put another way: women have feelings, men get erections. But you can be aroused long before your body gives you recognizable signs.

"There were bronze statuettes," John Updike writes in *Museums and Women*, "randomly burnished here and there as if by a caressing hand, of nudes and groups of nudes. I itched to finger them, to interact with them, to insert myself into their mysterious world. . . . They were in their smallness like secret thoughts of mine projected into dimension and permanence, and they returned to me as a response that carried strangely into parts of my body."

But not so strangely, of course. What we think and see returns to us as responses in our bodies.

On Trying Something New

Changing the way you make love with your partner is exciting in itself. New techniques, new attitudes, even choosing an unusual time of day or a new place to make love, all immeasurably enhance our enjoyment of sex. The old cliche is true: variety *is* the spice of life.

But breaking old habits can bring problems, too. You may find as you begin to experiment that you're more aroused than usual, and so you may ejaculate more quickly. Or the opposite could happen. Experimenting might distract you and cause you to lose your erection altogether. Don't worry. As you grow more comfortable with new techniques, the doubts and worries will fade, but the increased pleasure will remain. And don't hurry yourself. Sex isn't a race, and the only person watching over your shoulder is you.

Heightening Sensual Pleasure

"I feel your soft skin and I am excited.
I like the warm touch of your hand against my
chest. I see the glint of your earrings.
I run my hand down your neck and
my fingers caress your breasts.
I feel your nipples getting hard
and I feel your arms around me.
You're touching me gently in the middle of
my back and I'm getting aroused. I feel
how much I love you and being here with you.
I think how beautiful your body is,
how wonderful you look in this light.
I love the way your breasts look,
all pink and flushed. I'm tingling
as your hair brushes against my face.
I am getting on top of you now
and I want to enter. I am more excited,
my erection is getting harder, I want to move
into you and feel you around my penis."

This is a man fully experiencing the present. In bed with his lover, he's aware of his thoughts, his emotions, and his physical sensations. His body is real to him—he is attuned to how it feels. And he's taking joy in his partner's body, touching her, gazing at her.

You'll notice, too, what he's not doing. He isn't removing himself mentally from where he is. He isn't thinking about whether or not he'll get an erection, or anticipating his orgasm, or worrying about whether his partner is enjoying making love with him. He's not wondering whether the car needs to be washed or if the dry cleaner got the spot out of his favorite tie.

In short, he's alive in the act of sex. He's being both sexually and sensually excited, a distinction that matters. We usually think of sexual excitement as being registered in our genitals. Sensual feelings are those that reflect all of our senses—touch, smell, taste, hearing, sight; they differ from sexual feelings, but are an integral part of them, too.

One man swears that in the midst of making love he can call to mind and mentally linger over statistics from the 1976 Olympic Games and still have a wonderful sexual experience. He's a charming guy, very funny, successful in his career. But one has to wonder about what he considers satisfying sex. "The divorce between soul and body," Norman O. Brown wrote in *Love's Body*, "takes the life out of the body, reducing the organism to a mechanism, dead in itself but given an artificial life, an imitation of life, by will or power." To separate your emotions from your physical sensations, Brown is saying, is to purposely deny your own wholeness as a person. It is to be, in a way, dead, and it's the kind of split that by definition seems to make a complete sexual experience impossible.

Above the Belt, Below the Belt

In our culture we frequently separate love and lust. Love is above the belt, in the head and heart, and lust is below the belt, in the groin. We're able, or pretend to be able, to keep our emotions and our sexual drive separate. Part of our problem, as well an explanation for it, is the language we use to describe sex. We can talk, for example, about the physiology of sex as somehow isolated from the emotions we feel during sex. In fact, all of our language is shot through with distinctions that reinforce a mind/body duality. We acknowledge that when we're under stress, we're more apt to get sick; that's fine as far as it goes. But then we blithely explain that the mind affects the body, as if they were disconnected—the body in one room, the mind in another. Intuitively, though, we know that the mind and body aren't separate. Your mind and your body are always united in one organism—you.

We split ourselves artificially more than women do. We act out our love by buying our lovers perfume or jewelry, and we act out our lust by turning on sexually. We facetiously suggest that what would make a woman happy is raw sex divorced from feeling: "What she needs is a good fuck." In this case the joke reveals how uneasy we are about mixing sex with emotion.

Exactly why women are less inclined to separate love from sex is a bit of a mystery. In *The Sex Contract*, anthropologist Helen Fisher suggests that it might have something to do with the evolution of childbearing. When our earliest ancestors, the protohominids, learned to walk, the pelvis changed shape; in the process, the birth canal got smaller. Giving birth became more difficult. Fewer females could actually carry their young to delivery, and nature saw to it that those who could, had more than their share. No longer moving on hands and knees, females had to carry their young in their arms. Because they literally had their hands full, females began to depend more on males for food and protection. "Now females found it increasingly difficult to keep up with the daytime jaunt," Fisher writes, "to chase after small animals and join small hunting parties. Motherhood had become a grind. Females needed males to help them raise their children."

And so pairbonding was born—"the sex contract." With it came new emotions, kinship, and what we call civilization. Men often sneer at women's feelings —how easily they're moved, for example, by a gushy love song. But perhaps the inbred inability of women to separate sex and love gives them an advantage. Social psychologists argue that because women make this connection more strongly than men, they are emotionally healthier, more stable. They do cry when they are hurt, but as a consequence they may survive emotional pain better than we do.

Certainly men have the capacity to experience love and lust together. Indeed, we have the need to do so, but are boxed in by our conditioning, the roles we've been taught to play. One way to bring our minds as well as our bodies into bed—to stop dividing ourselves at the belt line—is to heighten our involvement in sex.

What's going on in your mind when you're aroused? What are you thinking about, what are you feeling, what are you imagining? Recent research by Drs. Julia Heiman and John Hatch at the State University of New York at Stonybrook revealed that men find the most satisfying sexual arousal not in the mere physical fact of an erection, but from arousal combined with sensuousness—the awareness of the sensations of closeness and touch and the desire for physical and emotional intimacy. Through sensual imagery, sensual awareness, and fantasies, we can reclaim our split selves and become whole.

Pictures at an Exhibition

Hundreds of images flash through our minds every day. We carry our own art galleries inside our brains. You might be driving to work and see in your mind's eye another car, perhaps the first car you can remember your family owning. Over dinner with your lover you might see the first time you met, literally see the colors of the room, the clothes she wore. Or you might have an altogether different picture, perhaps a beautiful woman in an ocean vista—a scene that you saw many years ago but that still haunts you today. And at night you dream, watching the reels of images assembled by your unconscious mind.

But the pictures in our heads aren't accidental; they're related to our thoughts and feelings. While laboratory research in human sexuality has concentrated on physiological responses, sex is obviously more than a penis engorging with blood or vascular changes that lubricate a vagina. The images in our mind are part of the sexual experience, too, and the chemical messengers of sex—hormones and neurotransmitters in the brain—partly determine how we feel. More important, the reverse is also true. How we feel affects the pictures we see.

107

We can see two kinds of pictures during sex: those that mentally reflect where we are and what we're doing, our sensual imagery; and those we make up, our fantasies. Both can enhance our experience of lovemaking and our technique.

The Enemy of Good Sex

Giving our full attention to any activity is difficult. We live in a hurried world, and we're always trying to do several things at once. Our minds are clouded with the myriad problems of daily life. While we eat, we also talk. While we work or study, we're interrupted by dozens of distractions—the telephone, the demands of a co-worker, the nagging worry that it's raining and the car windows are open.

That's the modern condition, and most of the time there just isn't much we can do about it. But distraction is the enemy of good sex. How can we give ourselves over to all the sensations and feelings of sex if we're not "there"—if we're not immersed in the experience? Equally important, how can we enjoy the emotional or physical intimacy of sex if we're busy watching ourselves in the act?

The poet Samuel Coleridge put the problem this way: "In dreams I do not recollect the state of feeling, so common when awake, of thinking of one subject and looking at another." What he meant is that when we dream, we're rarely aware that we're dreaming; we are *in* the dream. But often when we're awake, we're doing one thing and thinking another. In a dream we float through the action as it happens, but in life we stand back and watch ourselves. Psychologists have observed that some people, when they're self-conscious, don't remember the name of a person to whom they've just been introduced. When you're worrying about the impression you're making, when you're watching *you*, you won't even hear the other person's name.

Sports psychologists have discovered that similar problems afflict athletes. But the most successful professionals, they find, have developed maneuvers to make themselves concentrate on their game and screen out the distractions of self-consciousness. Now the sports doctors are turning what they've learned into new techniques for relaxation and staying in the moment.

In the psychological flux of competition—the fear of losing, the pressure to win, the normal anxiety of performance—many athletes lose voluntary control over their bodies. A "fight or flight" reaction sets in, the muscles tighten, and all the long hours of preparation are wasted as the mind and body in unison lose contact with the game. "With increased levels of arousal, attention begins to narrow," says Robert M. Nideffer, a professor at the California School of Professional Psychology in San Diego and an expert in the psychology of sports training. "This reduction in processing ability results in a feeling of being rushed. The athlete jumps from one thought to another, adding to his feeling of confusion. The person becomes distracted by his negative thoughts, and the ability to concentrate on the game deteriorates."

The solution, say the sports psychologists, is to help athletes focus on their experience, aware of how they undermine their own self-confidence, and gain control over their feelings. Mental imagery promotes concentration, and breathing exercises promote relaxation. What coaches and players are beginning to understand, and a few great athletes have probably always understood, is that playing a game well calls for both mental and physical conditioning.

See, Feel, and Do: Immersing Yourself in the Moment

Go back now and look at the beginning of this chapter—at the man who is entirely involved in making love with his partner. This may not be the way you feel during sex. But you can learn to stay with your senses by trying to see, feel, and do.

Let's start with "see." One way to see is to keep your eyes closed and mentally look at what's happening. As your partner touches you, try to envision her hand against your skin. As your penis enters, try to see it penetrate the opening of the vagina.

Another way to see is to keep your eyes open. Many of us are accustomed to making love with the lights out, and even in the dark we close our eyes. The next time you make love, notice what happens if you keep your eyes open more than usual. You'll probably find this strange at first. You might become more aroused by the sight of your partner's naked body. You're also likely to be self-conscious just by virtue of trying something different. But you might eventually discover that seeing your partner helps keep you immersed in the enjoyment of sex.

You'll be more aware, too, of the physical sensations of sex, and that's part of "feel." During intercourse you can be aware of how your hips are swinging as you begin to move back and forth. Are your partner's arms around you? How do her hands feel on your back? Focus on the sensations in your penis. What does the wetness of the vagina feel like? Maybe in the past when your partner stroked your penis too roughly, you tried to ignore the discomfort, hoping she'd stop. But if you're actively involved in the sexual experience, you'll find a way to communicate your feelings—by taking her hand, perhaps, and moving it more gently.

You'll notice smells, too. Among animals, smell —usually emitted by the female to attract the male—is a primary stimulus of sexual interest. Although in humans smell is less significant than sight, our bodies do give off scents called pherenomes, unique to each person, and smell undoubtedly plays some role in why a man initially attracted to a particular woman. To see just how much sexual power is attributed to smell, glance through any magazine or check the perfume counter at your local department store. Artificial aromas are fine sometimes, but during sex nature's own olfactory department turns us on far more powerfully. During intercourse, drawing in your partner's natural perfume will add to your arousal.

Feeling also refers to your emotions. Do you hear yourself saying, "I'm not enjoying this because she's moving too fast," or "I'll bet she's bored"? Respond to those feelings. In the first case, slow down; your partner will adjust to your rhythm. In the second, retrain yourself to move away from negative thoughts. Why not assume she's experiencing pleasure? When you start to get distracted ("Is she enjoying this? Am I going to come too quickly?"), then consciously steer yourself back to the here and now. Stay with how your body feels. Stay with the sensations of the moment.

Let your inner voice talk about your enjoyment.

This is where the "do" comes in. When you're actively engaged in "see" and "feel," you'll more naturally do what you'd like. If during intercourse, for example, you'd like your partner to caress your testicles, reach around, find her hand, and move it the way you'd like to be stroked. If you have a sudden urge to roll over, say, and have your partner on top, start rolling and see what happens. Your partner may have been thinking the same thing, or she may not, but either way she'll let you know. On the other hand, if you're honestly tired, feel free to say so.

By staying with yourself and your partner in the moment, you're also liable to discover that you haven't been getting some of what you want and need during sex. Because you'll be increasingly aware of tactile sensations, you might find, as many men do, that you'd like to be touched more. If you're not determined to rush headlong to orgasm, either yours or hers, you may want to have your back stroked or simply cuddle for a while. And you may want to touch your partner's body more leisurely, without moving so quickly to her genitals.

Men generally aren't comfortable with their own need to be touched, and consequently we're restrained in our physical affection toward everyone else, including our lovers. We may think it's our job to do the touching and caressing—another by-product of the provider role—but primarily we focus on a woman's breasts and genitals. The idea of being touched very much ourselves, sexually or otherwise, makes many of us particularly uneasy. We ritualize our need for human contact in sports, and even in the simple act of shaking hands, which was once man's way of showing he carried no weapon and came as a friend. But we carry over this conditioning to sex by relegating most touching to "below the belt."

Because of the nerve endings in our skin, touch conveys continuous sensual messages to the brain. When you see, feel, and do, you're much more receptive to the pleasurable sensations touch can bring.

Finally, you can pay attention to what's going on inside your body—particularly, as mentioned on page 89 , your breathing. A psychiatrist voiced an interesting theory as to why some people smoke cigarettes even after they've long since tired of the taste and want to quit: they feel out of touch with their bodies, or emotionally out of control, and use smoking to sense and control their breathing as a method for getting connected again. The process of inhaling and expelling smoke becomes a sensual experience.

But you don't need smoke in your lungs for breathing to be sensual. By being aware of how you breathe during intercourse, by feeling your lungs move, you'll transmit the sensation to the rest of your body. As your sexual tension grows, your breathing changes. When you feel your breathing begin to speed up, for example, you'll know you're on the path to orgasm. If you want to slow your pace toward orgasm, you can consciously slow your breathing; you'll relax your body but stay aroused and remain in the experience. Paying attention to how you breathe also heightens your other sensual feelings.

The next time you have intercourse, try these three simple steps. One, begin by being aware of only your physical sensations. Pay particular attention to touch and smell. What does your body feel—your chest, lungs, arms, penis, testicles, legs, feet? Two, open your eyes and take pleasure in your partner, in how much you enjoy being with her and the sensual experience you're enjoying together. Don't make judgments. Don't worry about your orgasm. Do what you want to do. And three, let the imagery of sex fill your mind—your penis, your testicles, the curling hair of your partner's labia, her clitoris, her vagina, your entry into her, your bodies meshing together. Stay with those feelings as continuously as you can. Sometimes you'll be distracted. Just return your focus to the moment.

Training yourself to "see, feel, and do" isn't difficult. It's very much like meditation or yoga; the essence of both is remaining in the moment with no goal other than relaxation. In some forms of meditation a single word is repeated mentally again and again as a technique to relax the body and empty the mind. Distracting thoughts do creep in, but the sound of the single repeated word continues to flow through one's consciousness. "See, feel, and do" also relies on the Zen idea that the only way to reach any goal is to go one step at a time. An archer who is thinking only about aiming for the target will undoubtedly miss. An archer who takes care as he positions the arrow, feels the tautness of the bow, and experiences his muscles tensing under the pressure isn't actually aiming for the target at all; he's engaged in the process of shooting an arrow.

"See, feel, and do" isn't a trick and implies no goal beyond relaxing and enjoying the moment. If your goal in sex is reaching orgasm as quickly as possible, "see, feel, and do" won't work. But if you want to share and experience mutual pleasure, it will.

The Images of Eros

In ancient mythology the god Eros was born, appropriately enough, out of Chaos, the Greeks' name for the original void. Love was part of the creation of the universe. Of all the heavenly deities Eros was the most beautiful. His gold-tipped arrow caused man and god alike to fall in love. From Eros' name comes the word "erotic," our catchall term for the sexual feelings and fantasies associated with love.

For most of us, fantasies in some form are inseparable from arousal. Sometimes you'll see clear pictures in your head, your own home movies; sometimes the images will be vague. They can arise spontaneously, or you can voluntarily create them. A fantasy might appear unbidden from memory—a remembered sexual experience—or be entirely imaginary. Studies show that most men fantasize to one degree or another during masturbation, and that, although you might not be aware of them, fantasies often play a large role when you're aroused by your partner. In your mind you may be watching her undress, and the image alone will be enough to put you in the mood for lovemaking. With a woman you've just met, you may be more conscious of the pictures in your mind. She might evoke the idea, along with an image, of your being in bed together. Or you might fantasize a specific scenario of seduction. Whatever the image, you can become sexually aroused within a matter of seconds. The mere sight of a woman can call up a fantasy that stirs both your heart and your penis.

But our fantasies serve as more than an instant trigger for erection. They allow us to mentally play with desires we wouldn't think of acting out in life. The fantasy is the turn-on, and the fantasy is enough. Your fantasies can also tell you about yourself, about what you want from sex. You might have a recurrent fantasy, for example, of being ravished by a woman; this might mean you'd like your partner to be more aggressive, or at least for her to initiate sex more frequently and passionately than she does.

Sex researchers and psychologists alike seem to agree that all of us have what are called primary fantasies, probably coded into our "love map" when we're very young, perhaps even before puberty. Some people add primary fantasies when they're older, especially if they've broken through taboos against expressing their sexuality or if their earlier fantasies in some way fail to meet their emotional needs.

Throughout our lives we elaborate on our primary fantasies, adding new images in specific situations, depending on our mood and our partner. But the content of our essential fantasies—the ideas and images that turn us on most—rarely changes. If you've occasionally been excited by the idea of many women desiring you, chances are the same fantasy will occur again and again.

What you find arousing won't necessarily be stimulating to someone else. Most men, for example, find the sight of a scantily clad woman more arousing than complete nudity. But some men are turned on by a woman's breasts, others by the curve of a leg or another part of the body. How often we have fantasies also varies widely. The majority of men, according to one recent survey, report having an erotic fantasy at least once a day. This might be nothing more than a fleeting thought—the idea of a sexual encounter, say, with a woman sitting nearby in a restaurant.

Among men's most common erotic fantasies are kissing a woman's genitals, seeing a specific part of a woman's body, reliving a previous sexual experience, and having sex with a woman other than the regular partner or with many women at the same time. Many men have a broader range of fantasies, such as being seduced by a woman who teaches them about sex, "kinky" sex of one sort or another, and group sex. Sometimes, particularly when we masturbate, we create elaborate scenarios. We might envision a lengthy scene where we meet a woman, talk with her, go to a bedroom, and either seduce her or be seduced by her. In some fantasies women are adoring and totally passive; they want you to do everything, and respond ecstatically when you oblige. In other fantasies women are passionately aggressive, taking the lead and devoting themselves to your pleasure, or to their own.

Some of us don't like to admit that we have certain fantasies. We judge ourselves negatively if we're aroused by images we consider wrong or bad. Fantasies reported by men to Nancy Friday for her book *Men in Love* included scenes of intercourse with animals, men watching their lovers and wives penetrated by men with enormous penises, capturing women and turning them into sex slaves, and watching one's partner make love to another woman. Because we wouldn't find these pastimes acceptable in real life, it may be difficult for us to acknowledge that the idea is a turn-on. But no fantasy in and of itself is bad or good. What's important is how you react. Why not let yourself enjoy your fantasies for what they are

—the waking equivalent of dreams? Fantasies can, of course, be troublesome if they take the place of actual sex, if you're too involved in your fantasies to appreciate an intimate sexual experience. Like fantasies about everything else, what you can imagine about sex sometimes surpasses real-life experience. And if your fantasies make you uncomfortable, they can get in the way of your enjoyment.

But fantasies have a healthy and vital role to play in our experience of sex. A recent study at the University of Quebec in Montreal, for example, shows just how effectively fantasies can enhance both technique and pleasure. The researchers discovered that men who have fantasies during sex are more capable of choosing when they reach orgasm. These men also felt less anxiety during sex and could better appreciate and enjoy their own excitement.

For this reason alone, you may want to explore your own fantasies, especially during sex. Some men feel guilty about having fantasies during intercourse; they wonder why their partner isn't enough. It's true that if you consistently need fantasies of other women to reach orgasm, something is lacking in your relationship. But you can create mental pictures combining sensual imagery and fantasy to heighten your levels of arousal before orgasm. During intercourse visualize yourself and your partner in the act. Stay with that image until the tide of sensations sweeps you over the edge to orgasm.

You may want to share some of your fantasies with your partner. This is difficult for most of us and requires some delicacy. But if you'd like to try something new, a specific scenario you've fantasized, the best way to see if she's interested is to tell her. Remember that women, too, have fantasies; ask her about her's. When you share yours, she may feel less inhibited about revealing her own.

Focusing For Feeling

The following three exercises bring together sensual, sexual, and emotional feelings. They're meant to be done as a sequence, giving you greater awareness of how you feel during sex—how your arousal builds —and thus allowing you to recondition your delay reflex. Staying aware of your physical sensations alerts you to your pace toward orgasm, while manipulating the PG-point lets you alter the pace.

Do the exercises alone at first and then with your partner's help during intercourse. If you're not comfortable suggesting changes to your partner, you might ask her to read the instructions for these exercises, too. She'll very likely be more than happy to help you increase both your pleasure and your control.

You'll probably respond to these exercises with new and different sensations. At first you might ejaculate more quickly than usual, especially when you find yourself so aroused by focusing that you're swept away by the flood of sensations leading to orgasm. As you learn how you feel when you approach your own moment of no return—the sensation of ejaculatory inevitability—you'll develop more control.

1. Sensual Awareness for Delay

This exercise concentrates on sensual awareness. It's important to stay with your moment-to-moment physical sensations and try not to evoke sensual imagery or fantasy.

Begin by masturbating until you start to grow erect. Locate the areas of your Y-zone where touching stimulates you to erection most quickly and the areas to which you give the most attention as you feel the urge to ejaculate. The idea is to become aware of how you bring yourself to orgasm, without losing your erection at the same time. Focusing on the sensations in the Y-zone gives you an opportunity to stay sexually aroused without distractions.

Notice how your body feels as you grow more aroused. How does your breathing change? Is the corona of your penis more sensitive? When do you begin to stroke more rapidly, and where do you concentrate the motion? Can you feel the shaft beginning to pulse? You'll feel yourself reaching ejaculatory inevitability when your pelvic muscles start to tense, your scrotum tightens, and your testicles begin to rise.

Before you ejaculate, stop, relax, and start again. (If you stopped too late and ejaculated, start the exercise again at another time, trying to again sense your moment of ejaculatory inevitability.) As you start again, press hard on your PG-point and see whether the pressure is arousing or inhibitory and how it changes. Then, as your arousal builds, you can begin conditioning your delay reflex. As you continue masturbating, try to pinpoint your moment of ejaculatory inevitability. Pay particular attention to your breathing, your heart rate, and the subliminal contractions of your pelvic muscles. Press on your PG-point as you feel yourself approaching ejaculation.

Repeat the exercise until you've grown aware of your most sensitive stimulation locations. Repeating this several times completes the first step in conditioning the delay reflex.

2. Sensual Awareness, Sensual Imagery, and Delay

In this second exercise, you add sensual imagery to sensual awareness. When you're aroused, begin focusing mentally on the image of your erect penis—what it looks like, the motions you're making with your hands, where you're touching yourself. Visualize how your body moves in response to arousal. Stay attuned to the physical feeling and the sensual imagery as well as the pleasure you're giving yourself.

You'll probably find that you want to ejaculate more quickly when you add sensual imagery to sensual awareness, both while masturbating and during intercourse. Now, because you've begun to condition the delay reflex, you can use the PG-point to delay your orgasm while continuing to visualize sexual imagery. When you feel the urge to ejaculate, continue focusing on the image of your penis, but manipulate the PG-point to slow your pace to orgasm.

When you try this exercise during intercourse, let your partner know you're trying to control the timing of your orgasm, and tell her what you've learned. Ask her to touch those areas you find most arousing until you feel your muscles begin to contract and you sense that you're going to ejaculate. Then ask her to manipulate the PG-point as you did while masturbating. As both you and your partner grow accustomed to using the PG-point, your partner will be able to help you delay and also to increase your sexual tension as a prelude to orgasm.

3. Sensual Awareness, Sensual Imagery, Fantasy, and Delay

This exercise adds fantasy to sensual awareness and imagery. Repeat the steps in the previous exercises leading to arousal and ejaculatory inevitability. This time try to envision your partner; actively imagine her caresses, her face, the touch of her skin on yours. Mentally act out having sex with her. Fantasize how you would make love, specifically whatever you and your partner might do. This might include oral sex, your partner masturbating you, various kinds of touching and stroking. Carry the fantasy to visualizing your penis entering her vagina and the motions you would make. See which visions of your partner and which kinds of touch lead you most quickly to orgasm.

When you have the urge to ejaculate, touch your PG-point in the ways you've already learned in order to slow down, but continue with the fantasy. Be aware of the pleasurable sensations of intercourse. You may ejaculate sooner than you'd like, but with practice you'll condition the delay reflex so that you can imagine penetration as well as moving in and out and stay aroused without reaching orgasm. Trying a mental replay when you have sex with your partner will allow you to stay with your sensual feelings and more clearly identify what leads you to orgasm.

When making love with your partner, incorporate all three exercises in the same order. She will be able to manipulate your PG-point to help you delay. You'll find, too, that once you've begun to train the delay reflex, you and your partner may want to vary the texture of your lovemaking—the times you choose to have sex, the ways in which you stimulate each other, the positions you use —because changes won't be so arousing that you ejaculate before you want to.

Two People

There is one more exercise. This is the last in the pages of this book. It takes only a few minutes and it's easy. First, without reflecting on, or weighing the words that come to mind, close your eyes and think of the words and phrases you've heard from other men, and used with other men, in describing intercourse. Then close your eyes again and allow yourself to remember the sensations of loving sex when you've cared deeply and honestly for your partner.

Is it the articulated language or the remembered sensations that best define the reality of sensual intimacy? To most of us, the truth is in the fully realized experience where emotions and physical sensations blend into a single, all-encompassing experience, transcending language. Such moments are possible only when physical abilities and emotional involvement are not

only equal partners but are woven together and become a complete experience.

That is a state, an important and an exhilarating part of your life, that can become more than a rare and accidental occurance. Getting in touch with your own body, breathing fully in order to maximize your physical and emotional sensitivity, and understanding the physiology of intercourse are the means to laying down a foundation for an emotional and lasting bond between two people.

And there is one more question. You might try answering it not with words but with feelings, with your entire being. Ask yourself, "What do I love, who do I love?" And then get on with it.

Bibliography

Barbach, Lonnie, *For Each Other: Sharing Sexual Intimacy.* Garden City: Anchor Press/Doubleday (1982).

Beltrami, Edouard, "Orgasm and Ecstasy: Neurophysiological Differences," *British Journal of Sexual Medicine* (April 1982).

Bohlen, Joseph G., Held, James P., and Sanderson, Margaret Olwen, "The Male Orgasm: Pelvic Contractions Measured by Anal Probe," *Archives of Sexual Behavior,* 9:6 (1980).

Bohlen, Joseph G.; Held, James P.; Sanderson, Margaret Olwen; and Ahlgren, Andrew, "The Female Orgasm: Pelvic Contractions," *Archives of Sexual Behavior,* 11:5 (1982).

Brauer, Alan P., and Brauer, Donna, *ESO: How You and Your Lover Can Give Each Other Hours of Extended Sexual Orgasm.* New York: Warner (1983).

Brown, Norman O., *Love's Body. New York: Vintage* (1966).

Campbell, H.J., *The Pleasure Areas. New York: Delacorte* (1973).

Crêpault, Claude and Couture, Marcel, "Men's Erotic Fantasies," *Archives of Sexual Behavior,* 9:6(1980).

Derogatis, Leonard, "Etiologic Factors in Premature Ejaculation," *Medical Aspects of Human Sexuality,* 14:6 (1980).

Fisher, Helen, *The Sex Contract: The Evolution of Human Behavior. New York: Quill* (1982).

Friday, Nancy, *Men In Love. Male Sexual Fantasies: The Triumph of Love Over Rage. (New York:* Delacorte *(1980).*

Graber, Benjamin, ed., *Circumvaginal Musculature and Sexual Function.* (New York: S. Karger,) 1982.

Graber, Benjamin, "Progress in Defining the Neurobiology of the Sexual System," in Hoch, Zwi and Lief, Harold I, eds., *Sexology: Sexual Biology, Behavior and Therapy: Selected Papers of the 5th World Congress of Sexology, Jerusalem, Israel, June 21–26, 1981.* –Amsterdam–Oxford–Princeton:Excerpta Medica, 1982.

————, "Circumvaginal Musculature and Female Sexual Function: The Past, Present and Future,"*Journal of Sex and Marital Therapy,* 7:1 (Spring 1981).

————, "Muscle Phenomena in Sexual Function and Dysfunction," unpublished paper presented at 5th World Congress of Sexology, Jerusalem, Israel, June 21–26, 1981.

————, "The Urge to Merge," unpublished paper presented at 6th World Congress of Sexology, Washington, D.C., 1983.

Graber, Benjamin; Blake, Charles; Gartner, Joseph; and Wilson, James E., "The Effects of Opiate Receptor Blockade on Male Sexual Response," unpublished paper presented at 6th World Congress of Sexology, Washington, D.C., 1983.

Graber, Benjamin and Kline-Graber, Georgia, "Research Criteria for Male Erectile Failure," *Journal of Sex & Marital Therapy,* 7:1 (Spring 1981).

————, "Diagnosis and Treatment Procedures of Pubococcygeal Deficiencies in Women," in LoPiccolo, Joseph and LoPiccolo, Leslie, eds., *Handbook of Sex Therapy.* New York: Plenum (1978).

Greenspan, Emily, "Conditioning Athletes' Minds," *New York Times Magazine* (August 28, 1983).

Hagen, Richard, *The Bio-Sexual Factor.* New York: Doubleday (1979).

Heiman, Julia R., and Hatch, John P., "Conceptual and Therapeutic Contributions of Psychophysiology to Sexual Dysfunction," in Haynes, S.N. and Gannon, L., eds., *Psychosomatic Disorders*. New York: Praeger (1981).

———, "Affective and Physiological Dimensions of Male Sexual Response to Erotica and Fantasy," *Basic and Applied Social Psychology*, 1:4 (1980).

Heiman, Julia R., and Verhulst, Johan, "Gender and Sexual Functioning," in *Gender and Psychopathology*. New York: Academic Press (1982).

Henderson, Harry, "The Evolution of Sex Therapy," *Sexual Medicine Today,* 5:5 (1981).

———, "Exploring the Human Sexual Response," *Sexual Medicine Today*, 5:4 (1981).

Hite, Shere, *The Hite Report*. New York: Dell (1977).

———, *the Hite Report on Male Sexuality*. New York: Knopf (1981).

Horowitz, Joseph, *Conversations with Arrau*. New York: Knopf (1982).

Jorgensen, Valerie, "A Woman's View of Men's Sexual Problems," *Medical Aspects of Human Sexuality*, 15:9 (1981).

Kaplan, Helen Singer, *The New Sex Therapy: Active Treatment of Sexual Dysfunctions*. New York: Brunner/Mazel-Times Books (1974).

Kelly, Gary F., *Good Sex: The Healthy Man's Guide to Sexual Fulfillment*. New York: Harcourt Brace Jovanovich (1979).

Kruse, Janet A., and Gottmann, John M., "Time Series Methodology in the Study of Sexual Hormonal and Behavioral Cycles," *Archives of Sexual Behavior*, 2:5 (1982).

Kwan, Marie; Greenleaf, Walter J.; Mann, Jay; Crapo, Lawrence; and Davidson, Julian M., "The Nature of Androgen Action on Male Sexuality: A Combined Laboratory-Self-Report Study on Hypogonadal Men," *Journal of Clinical Endocrinology and Metabolism*, 57:3 (1983).

Ladas, Alice Kahn; Whipple, Beverly; and Perry, John D., *The G Spot and Other Recent Discoveries About Human Sexuality*. New York: Holt, Rinehart and Winston (1982).

Leonard, George, *The End of Sex: Erotic Love After the Sexual Revolution*. Los Angeles: J.P. Tarcher (1983).

Lewis, Denslow, "The Gynecologic Consideration of the Sexual Act." *Journal of the American Medical Association*, 250:2 (1983).

LoPiccolo, Joseph and Friedman, Jerry M., "Sex Therapy: An Integrative Model," in Lynn, S.J., and Garske, J.P., eds., *Contemporary Psychotherapies: Models and Methods*. New York: Charles E. Merrill (1983).

Lowen, Alexander, *Bioenergetics*. New York: Penguin (1976).

———, *Pleasure*. New York: Penguin (1975).

———, *Love and Orgasm*. New York: Collier (1975).

Marcuse, Herbert, *Eros and Civilization*. New York: Vintage (1955).

Masters, William H., and Johnson, Virginia E., *Human Sexual Response*. New York: Bantam (1980).

———, *Human Sexual Inadequacy*. New York: Bantam (1980).

McCarthy, Barry, *What You Still Don't Know About Male Sexuality*. New York: Crowell (1977).

Money, John, "Clinical Frontiers and the Three Phases of Sexuality: Proception, Acception, and Conception," in Meade, Gordon H., ed., *Frontiers of Medicine*. New York: Plenum Press (1977).

———, "The Development of Sexuality and Eroticism in Humankind," *Quarterly Review of Biology*, 56:4 (1981).

————, "Sexosophy and Sexology, Philosophy and Science: Two Halves, One Whole," in Hoch, Zwi and Lief, Harold I, eds., *Sexology: Sexual Biology, Behavior, and Therapy: Selected Papers of the 5th World Congress of Sexology, Jerusalem, Israel, June 21-26, 1981.* Amsterdam-Oxford-Princeton: Excerpta Medica (1982).

Murphy, James M., "Sex Problems and Body Movement Therapy," *Journal of Sex Education and Therapy*, 3 (1977).

Murray, Linda, "The New Frontier of Sex Research," *Science Digest* (June, 1982).

Nathan, Robert S., "Are Men Really the Weaker Sex?" *Cosmopolitan*, 186:6 (1979).

Perry, John Delbert, and Whipple, Beverly, "Pelvic Muscle Strength of Female Ejaculators: Evidence in Support of a New Theory of Orgasm," *The Journal of Sex Research*, 17:1 (1981).

Pietropinto, Anthony, and Simenauer, Jacqueline, *Beyond the Male Myth: What Women Want to Know About Men's Sexuality.* New York: New American Library (1978).

Schmidt, Gunter, "Sex and Society in the Eighties," *Archives of Sexual Behavior*, 11:2 (1982).

Sexual Medicine Today, "Arousal: The Most Fragile Link in Human Sexual Response," 6:9 (1982).

————, "Developments in Sexual Research: Female Ejaculation Documented," 6:2 (1982).

————, "Developments: Sexual Dimorphism," 6:9 (September, 1982).

————, "Developments: Erections, What Causes Them?" 6:6 (June, 1982).

Silber, Sherman J., *The Male: From Infancy to Old Age.* New York: Scribner's (1981).

Sloan, Don, "The Dual Therapy Approach to the Treatment of Sexual Dysfunction," in Sciarra, John J., ed., *Gynecology and Obstetrics.* Philadelphia: Harper & Row (1983).

Trimmer, Eric, "Practical Problem Solving in Sexual Medicine: Premature Ejaculation," *British Journal of Sexual Medicine* (July, 1982).

Tullman, Gerald M.; Gilner, Frank H.; Kolodny, Robert C.; Dornbush, Rhea L.; and Tullman, Gail D., "The Pre- and Post-Therapy Measurement of Communications Skills of Couples Undergoing Sex Therapy at the Masters & Johnson Institute," *Archives of Sexual Behavior*, 10:2 (1981).

Updike, John, *Museums and Women and Other Stories.* New York: Knopf (1972).

Wagenvoord, James, and Bailey, Peyton, *Men: A Book for Women.* New York: Avon (1978).

————, *Women: A Book for Men.* New York: Avon (1979).

Walsh, Patrick C., and Donker, Pieter, "Impotence Following Radical Prostatectomy: Insight into Etiology and Prevention," *The Journal of Urology*, 128 (September 1982).

Zilbergeld, Bernie, *Male Sexuality: A Guide to Sexual Fulfillment.* New York: Bantam (1978).